Can Psychological, Ethical, Biological and Mathematical Perspectives on Consumer Behaviour offer
A New Model of Market Segmentation?

Preface

This book is derived from my dissertation work produced in fulfillment of my Master Degree in Marketing Management at the University of Central Lancashire, Preston/UK, in 2005. At the time I was awarded by the Chartered Institute of Marketing (cim.co.uk) the Prize for the best Marketing Master's Student of 2005, becoming so the first Brazilian ever to receive such a recognition.

Although the publishing of this book comes out years after my postgraduation, I still believe that it can provide the reader a unique approach to a critical analysis of what has been written and said about marketing throughout all these years. Please do not take this writing as pretentions or simply exhaustive. I humbly invite you to take this trip towards the possibility of widening our way of perceiving marketing. Thank you to come on board and have fun!

Marcilio Silva

Acknowledgments

I would like to thank my dissertation supervisor Terry Horne for his invaluable help throughout the writing process of my study. Also, I thank my family and friends who have believed in my capacity and who have often thought of me during my time abroad. Finally, I would like to thank Clare Paine for patiently listening to me when I needed to confront my ideas.

Contents

Chapter 1 - Introduction
5

Chapter 2 – Looking at Possible Methodologies
18

Chapter 3 – A Psychology Perspective
29

Chapter 4 - An Ethical Perspective
46

Chapter 5 - A Biological Perspective
71

Chapter 6 - A Mathematical Perspective
86

Discussion
98

Conclusions
112

Recommendations
115

Bibliography
121

Chapter 1

Introduction

In this chapter various definitions of marketing and marketing concepts are explored and their concern, or not, with ethics is highlighted. The potential usefulness of various possible perspectives through an association with a case study of Christians' likelihood to buy fair-trade products is considered, leading finally to the need for a methodology that could be employed to take simultaneously advantage of a number of perspectives. The need for a more useful approach is identified.

Concepts of consumers, brand image, customers' brand preference and/or loyalty, relationship marketing, the marketing mix (the 4 and 7Ps), culture role in marketing research, consumer buyer behaviour and Integrated Marketing Communications (IMC) have all been used widely within marketing literature (Chernatony & McDonald, 2005; Pickton & Broderick, 2005; Belch and Belch, 2004; Taylor et al, 2004; Silva, 2004; Jobber, 2004; Czinkota & Ronkainen,

2004; Ball & Machas, 2003; Kotler, 2003; Stokes, 2002; Christopher & Ballantyne, 2002; Lovelock & Wright, 2002; Bhaskaran & Hardley, 2002; Duncan, 2002; Hoffman & Bateson, 2002; Gummesson, 2001; Craig & Douglas, 2001; Steemkamp, 2001; Groenroos, 2000; Shiffman & Kanuk, 1999; Alreck & Settle, 1999; Ferrand & Pages, 1999; Gabbott & Hogg, 1997).

Although these concepts have often been addressed separately, they build up an interconnected body of knowledge of marketing. According to Middleton & Clarke (2001, pp. 23), the British Chartered Institute of Marketing defines marketing as *"The management process responsible for identifying, anticipating and satisfying customer requirements profitably, to meet organisational objectives"* – this definition and its principles are also found on organizations' websites such as www.consultancymarketing.co.uk and www.bcentral.co.uk. It would be therefore plausible to affirm that the ultimate concern of marketers (academics or professionals alike) is to find ways of attracting costumers/consumers to a determined product/service (be it a company's brand or product brand itself) in order to induce them to the final step of the decision-making process; the profitable purchase. This definition is somewhat handicap, as it implies that customers' wants and needs are part of the same cluster 'requirements. It does not therefore clearly dissociate in meaning the two psychological and social elements. In addition, it reduces organisational objectives to profitable outcomes, when marketing should also be a means to achieve organisational aims other than profits themselves. This definition also ignores a reality in which marketers often seek to 'create' 'needs and wants' in their target customers.

Although marketing has been used for ethical and social reasons, this has been largely in the promotion of aid, charity and social awareness campaigns such as in the case of the (such as 'Live8' concerts associated with the 'Make Poverty History' campaign, and Government advertising against 'driving and drinking' in Britain, for instance). However, promotion is only one aspect of marketing. From the social perspective it can be said that marketing is not fully used for not-for-profit causes. It seems to the author that research in marketing has mainly focused on the development of strategies to boost the financial returns of companies through the selling of products and services.

Ethically dubious approaches have been used within marketing profession. "...there are reasons to believe that there may be very little commercial reward in terms of consumer purchasing to be gained by behaving as an ethical marketer" (Carrigan & Attalla, 2001 pp.560). This ought not to be taken as a constraint or justification for marketers not to behave ethically. The author believes that making the right choices and acting with consideration and responsibility towards others should be an aim in itself, independently of financial outcomes. Furthermore, there is evidence that behaving ethically can increase a company's development and success, even in countries permeated by fierce political and trade corruption. A good example of it is Semco S.A. from Brazil (Killian & Perez, 1998; Semler, 1994)

According to Fineman (1999) in Carrigan & Attallan (2001 pp.561), "marketing is more profoundly value laden (Smith, 1995; Laczniack, 1993), and manipulates the consumer in anything but an innocent way...the act of purchase and exchange is what interests marketers; it is an end in itself, remote from its relationship to others interests and concerns – like privacy, pollution or resource scarcity". Similarly, O'Shaughnessy & O'Shaughnessy (2002), point out that advertising encourages the 'perversion' of values through implying that the ownership of goods soothes consumer's deepest levels of discontent. Notwithstanding, Yam-Tang & Chan (1998) highlight that people are becoming aware of the connections between environmental problems and everyday consumption items like clothing, food, housing and transport. Likewise, Fletcher (1990) in Carrigan et al (2004) suggests that differently from the 'self-focused consumer' of the 1970s and the 'acquisitive consumer' of the 1980s; today's consumers are more values focused. Supporting such arguments, according to Ethical Consumer (2003), "Ethical consumers have at the core of their agenda the desire to enhance their wellbeing through purchasing behaviour that avoids harming or exploiting humans, animals and the environment". Shaw & Clarke (1999) not only pinpoint that emergence of a 'highly principled group of "ethical" consumers' in the 1990s, but also that fair trade was one of the main concerns of such consumers. It is therefore plausible to affirm that it was based on reasons such the ones above that a new breed of ethically oriented products such as the ones which hold the label Fair Trade or Tradecraft have been introduced recently (www.fairtrade.org , www.newconsumer.org, www.traidecraftshop.co.uk), which has opened a challenging market to marketing professionals, and academics alike. The latter ones will increasingly be faced with the development of a different marketing approach that ought to consider many ethical and social issues, yet without necessarily discarding the possibility of financial returns and market competition.

Shaw & Clarke (1999) affirm that in spite of the increasing concern for ethical problems, little in-depth research has been done on this subject. Another subject which has been as much neglected in marketing research is religion. Delener (1994 pp.36) says that "despite the potential importance of the religion or religiosity constructs, any empirical investigation of these constructs in consumer behaviour has been rare". Approximately 20 years after his article was published, the author has struggled to find other articles addressing the same subject within marketing electronic journals such as Ingenta and Emerald, for instance.

The importance of religion lies in two main facts. Most of the population of the world do follow or practice a type of religion. According to Mintel Report (2005), Christians comprise the biggest religious group with a number of followers 'anywhere' between 1 and 2 billion (for instance, 50.6% of the British population are considered Christians); Muslims encompass approx. 1.4 billion people;

Hinduism followers reach a number around 900million; and Buddhism 500million people. Similarly, The United Religions Initiative on their website (www.uri.org.uk) offers valuable information about religions and their number of followers around the world (see the following table for further information about the number of Christian denominations and followers).

Founding	Modern Facts
Where: Judea (later called Palestine, Israel). **When:** 30 C.E. **By Whom:** Jesus of Nazareth. **Also Known As:** Christ, Emmanuel. **Important Texts:** the Bible, containing the Old Testament (Hebrew Bible), the Gospels, and letters from Christ's Apostles.	**Major Divisions:** African Indigenous, Anglican, Catholic, Eastern Orthodox, Protestant. **Where Found:** Primarily in Europe, the Americas, Australia, but also parts of Asia and southern Africa. **Population:** 2,000 million total: 1,000 million Catholics, 400 million Protestants, 240 million Eastern Orthodox, 110 million African Indigenous, 73 million Anglican, and others.

Table from the website uri.org.uk

The second and perhaps most important is the fact that religion is an aspect of culture, which has a strong influence on one's values, habits, attitudes, and lifestyle; this influence in turn has an impact on consumer behaviour (Delener,

1994). Therefore, marketers cannot have the luxury of ignoring such social aspect if they are to achieve a comprehensive understanding of consumers; be it locally or internationally.

Inasmuch as what has been said, this research finds its justification on the limited research in ethics and religion associated with marketing; the fact that the author of the present research is a practicing Christian Catholic with wide travelling experience around the world and long-lasting experience exchanges with Christians in some countries such as Argentina, Italy, Germany and England (which provides him with a deep understanding of his faith that in turn has been achieved through experiential and vicarious learning (Pickton & Broderick, 2005); the author's shared belief with Fineman's (1999) statement about marketing and also the author's wish to contribute with knowledge that will facilitate the emergence of a more ethically conscious marketing practice; moreover, on the premise that although Christians form the largest group of followers around the world, contrary to common sense, this may not necessarily mean that they are potentially a powerful marketing segment for fair trade products; finally, the on the premise that the concept Fair Trade has become more and more fashionable and the products carrying such labels have increasingly gained market share (Cowe & Williams, 2000) and therefore, research in this area is precedent.

On their article entitled "Belief formation in ethical consumer groups: an exploratory study", Shaw & Clarke (1999) indicate that religion was repeatedly mentioned as a positive normative influence and on the creation of awareness of fair-trade products. However, there are indications that the holding of positive beliefs and attitude towards ethical issues such as environment friendly or fair-trade products, does not necessarily lead to ethical behaviour (be it the buying of ethical products or boycott of products from unethical companies). Other elements such as product quality, availability and price and information access may hinder/encourage consumer decision-making on the choice of ethical products (Carrigan et al, 2004; Bahskaran & Hardley, 2002; Carrigan & Attallan, 2001; Shaw & Clarke, 1999; Yam-Tang & Chan, 1998).

It is based on what has been said above and the fact that fair trade goods are classified as ethical products that the main problem of this research arises. Would

Christians be more likely than non-Christians to buy products which hold fair trade labels?

It can be said that because the Catholic Church is the oldest institution in the west side of the world (Stanford, 2005) and so, the Catholic denomination was the first group of Christians to emerge some 2000 years ago; the other denominations such as the Anglicans, Methodists and so forth were deeply influenced by its teachings - for the purpose of this study excerpts and concepts from a Christian Catholic Catechism Book has been used. Moreover, there still are elements commonly shared by the denominations' doctrines such as 'The Ten Commandments' (see any Bible from the different denominations) - these are the main teaching guidelines for people who want to live as Christians. Amongst the Commandments, the second, fourth, fifth and seventh ones are the most relevant for the research here proposed, as they provide Christians with their duties as citizens and attitudinal guidelines within society. They are respectively: 'You shall love your neighbour as yourself'; 'Honour your father and mother, that your days may be long in the land which the Lord your God gives you'; 'You shall not kill'; and 'You shall not steal' (Chapman, 1994). For instance, the fifth

Commandment preaches about the respect for human life and the respect for the dignity of the persons (e.g. respect for health); the seventh preaches about the respect for persons and their goods and economic activity and social justice (e.g. the obligation of business enterprises to consider the good of persons and not only profits; and the payment of just wages), and justice and solidarity among Nations as well as love for the poor.

As suggested before, religion can be a powerful influence on people's beliefs, habits, attitudes and lifestyle. If so, considering the depth of Christian teachings briefly above described, it would be plausible to affirm that because of the influence of Christian doctrine, Christians would therefore be more likely to buy fair-trade products than non-Christians.

Given the purpose of this research and the interest of the author in deepening his knowledge on philosophical research, the methodology adopted was based on critical thinking. The method is iterative, subjecting relevant information to reflective, creative, and critical thinking in order to generate inferences and draw conclusions (Horne & Wootton, 2005). Four main bodies of knowledge are thought likely to hold information relevant to the relationship between Christianity, fair trade and consumer behaviour. The bodies of knowledge selected for examination are psychology, ethics, biology and mathematics. Any attempt to bring together insights from four such different perspectives is problematic. Other possible methodologies were also considered as shown in the next chapter.

Given the emerging importance of concerns about the marketing of ethical products like fair-trade goods and the author's personal experience as a Christian and interest about the role played by religion on consumer behaviour, the initial aim of the research was tentatively framed as: to learn to think more critically about the implicit assumptions which underpin marketing in general and market segmentation in particular, by thinking through a particular Case Study of the role of Christianity in Fair Trade.

Given that many of the taken-for-granted assumptions in marketing are those that underpin the multi-disciplinary origins of marketing theory, the following objectives were set in furtherance of the overall research aim:

1. To critically review four main bodies of knowledge (Psychology, Ethics, Biology and Mathematics) and interrelate the case study of Christians' likelihood to buy fair trade products to these bodies of knowledge's theories
2. To generate inferences relevant to marketing knowledge
3. To offer sound conclusions from the inferences generated
4. To offer a way forward for marketing knowledge and practice

Chapter 2

Looking at Possible Methodologies

Chapter 1 introduced the potential paradox of marketers – at best secular and amoral practitioners – appealing to the moral and ethical values of others. In order to expose that paradox, and perhaps resolve some of the dilemma, the case study on marketing fairly traded goods to Christians is proposed. Bodies of knowledge from psychology, ethics, biology and mathematics might be sources of insight; but how to find a methodology that could bring together such disparate perspectives?

According to Giddens cited by Hughes (1990), there are four basic claims that underlie the positivism. "First, that reality consists in what is available to the senses. Second, philosophy, while a distinct discipline is parasitic on the findings of science…Third, that the natural and the human sciences share common logical and methodological foundations…Fourth, that there is a fundamental distinction between fact and value, science dealing with the former while the latter belonging to an entirely different order of discourse beyond the remit of science". Based upon the statement above it is possible to reach the conclusion that in the positivism perspective reality is seen in its permanent state without the interference of the human beings. Reality is not the result of human interactive and constructive process, but it is the result of rational responses influenced by social laws (Sarantakos, 1998). The emphasis here is that knowledge is to be discerned, understood and classified without recurring to the human consciousness. According to the positivist viewpoint everyone sees the world in the same way as if a superior social norm ruled all other 'sub-norms' and therefore, determined the perception of reality. As a result, every event is seen in the same way by people and has the same meaning and consequently, human behaviour is inevitably pre-shaped and predictable. This leads to the conclusion that everything we do is not a result of our personal choice, but a result of what it was predicted to be according to what has been imposed to us by social norms. Positivism in social research is concerned about finding within a subgroup congruent answers which could lead to posterior generalization of a specific analysed event as being representative for the main group. All this, based upon the predictability of a phenomena and the objectivity of the researcher. As mentioned by May (2001) "the social scientist must study social phenomena 'in the same state of mind as the physicist, chemist or physiologist when he probes into a still unexplored region of the scientific domain' (Durkheim 1964: xiv)." In the positivist approach deductive reasoning is the logical process and quantitative methodology is applied through methods such as the survey and analysis of data based on statistics (Saunders et al, 1997). "Quantitative methodology is based on the positivist or neopositivist philosophy..." (Sarantakos, 1998) – these previous assumptions sit unhappily alongside the research concerns expressed in the previous chapter 1. The author, firstly, believes that human behaviour cannot be treated in the light of natural sciences alone, since it can vary through environmental influences that in turn can also not be completely controlled (see chapter 5). Secondly, knowledge cannot be discerned, understood and classified without the personal worldview of researchers and their conscience. To assume that positivist research and researchers are entirely beyond the influence of their personal standpoints and interpretations is so unreasonable that it threatens their own validity and reliability, especially given that positive research applied in social sciences is not only carried out by human beings (and the deductive reasoning is applied by these very same human beings, which inevitably makes their inputs partial), but also it has as its subject human beings, who themselves may interfere and influence the findings of a research.

The interpretive paradigm comes with a different way of seeing reality from that of the positivist. Reality within this perspective is not a static, but a dynamic process influenced by human beings' interactions with their social environment, resulting in a construction of knowledge which has its origins in common sense (Denzin & Lincoln, 2000). May (2001), highlights that social life and social events are not explained by science, but by common sense which is related to the people's understanding of their lives. Reality is described in a symbolic way and knowledge is derived from understanding meanings and interpretations rather than only derived through the senses. Thus, science is in this case is assumed to be influenced by personal values.

As the name already indicates, the interpretive paradigm is concerned about the way events take place, why they take place in a specific way and what determines them. According to Crotty (1998) this epistemological stance is related to Max Weber's thought about the concern of human sciences in understanding (zu verstehen – in German) reality rather than explaining (zu erklaeren) it. Saratankos (1998) affirms that research based on the interpretive perspective helps to interpret and understand people's reasons for their social actions, the meanings they attach to their lives and their social context. Crotty (1998) emphasizes that throughout history the interpretive approach has been present in different streams such as symbolic interactionism, phenomenology and hermeneutics. For instance, in the symbolic interactionism stance a methodology commonly used is the Ethnography (Denzin & Lincoln, 2000), which according to Crotty (1998 pp7) "...seeks to uncover the meanings and perceptions on the part of people participating in the research, viewing these understandings against the backdrop of people's overall worldview or 'culture'. In line with this approach the researcher strives to see things from the perspective of the participants". Because "only through dialogue can one become aware of the perceptions, feelings and attitudes of others and interpret their meanings and intent" (Crotty, 1998 pp 75), usually the methods chosen for ethnographic studies are the participant observation as well as the in-depth interviews (Padgett, 1998) (which can further be subdivided into 'structured', 'semi-structured' and 'unstructured' (May, 2001) or 'semi standardized' and 'no standardized' (Berg, 2001)). Participant observation is a method that involves social interaction between the researcher and the participants of the research; "...the idea being to allow the observer to first-hand the day-to-day experience and behaviour of subjects in particular situations, and, if necessary, to talk to them about their feelings and interpretations" (Waddington (2004) in Cassel & Symon, 2004). Independently on which approach of the interpretive paradigm is used, there always exist the assumption that the people involved in the research process, their way of conceiving their social function and the world are of extreme importance for the final outcome, given that reality is the product of those people's interactions with the environment and vice versa. Rather than utilizing only the deductive reasoning, which would start from theoretical explanations of events to specific hypothesis about them; inductive reasoning is the logical starting process used in interpretive research. Inductive reasoning is based upon specific observations that are tested hypothetically in order to build the general theory about a certain event (Thomas & Nelson, 1996).

The interpretive perspective looks at the variability of reality, its determinants and its dynamic starting from the principle that there is no final predictable result standing as a product of exclusive sensorial interpretation of knowledge. Instead, the result can vary according to the level of interaction between the phenomena studied, its environment and its conditioning influence on the interpretation of knowledge. Here the qualitative approach is used rather than the quantitative as "it tries to capture reality in interaction" and "it uses no quantitative measures and variables" (Sarantakos, 1998).

Denzin's, in Seale (2000), observations about qualitative approach in post-modern society claims that by making qualitative research scientifically respectable academics may come to interpretations that simplify or do not fit that world as it is a result of the influence of interacting individuals – the author believes that more than simplifying reality, qualitative research rather highlights the complexity of the social phenomena and admits that there is no research approaches that are not passive of human influences and personal bias. In addition, without denying the importance of accurate methodological schemes (e.g. statistical analysis) and impartiality in research in order to achieve (as much as possible) an understanding of reality as it is, one cannot underestimate the potential of the qualitative approach, given that to interpret social reality through pure statistics quantifications of data it is here believed not to be the most accurate and exhaustive way of assessing the human universe and its variations. Inasmuch as what has been said, qualitative research on its own has its limitations as well, as its findings can neither be applicable generally (as its samples usually are not representative enough), nor can its findings be moderated by controlled variables.

On the one hand, the quantitative approach (e.g. positivist and neo-positivist paradigms; surveys; statistical analysis) through methods such as structured surveys and probabilistic/statistical analysis provides the researchers with a great amount of data based on which findings can be generalized to a whole population and a straightforward answers for very specific questions may be achieved - although the 'general picture' can be reached through such approach, it lacks of a deeper understanding of social phenomena; the 'whys' related to it remain without answers. Therefore, in the case of consumer behaviour (for example), its findings may be misleading, as without a deep understanding of the real reasons why people behave in a specific way, marketers end up like foreigners who cannot speak the native language of a country: they see what is around; perceive that some events happen regularly in different places in similar ways; however, they are unable to explain why, since they cannot blend culturally and they cannot interact with and ask natives about their reasons for acting that way. On the other hand, the qualitative approach (e.g. interpretive paradigm, participant observation and in-depth interviews) may offer a more in-depth understanding of social phenomena, it may offer the answers for the 'whys' about human behaviour, however, only of those people involved in the research process. Research that uses such approach lacks of a general view of the 'picture'. This way, marketers end up becoming like natives of a community who understand the reasons why they behave in a certain way, about their beliefs and the elements that influence their behaviour (since marketers would have an insight from within). Nonetheless, given that they become so immersed in one reality they may lose the capacity to see beyond that specific world; they tend to become somewhat narrow minded and miss what is happening beyond their horizons.

Given that there is not one research approach in the social sciences that can be claimed to be exhaustive and absolutely accurate, also that there is no research design which does not suffer from their own weaknesses and from personal bias.

Considering still that human behaviour can neither be understood and explained through only statistical analysis, nor can its general understanding be reduced to a specific group of studied people and that the author believes that humans' worldview and interpretations of social phenomena are biased by personal and social influences (therefore, it may be determined by such influences). Also considering that a positivist approach to human behaviour is here believed to be virtually misleading. In addition, the author believes that reality can only be comprehensively interpreted with the contributions and interactions of different standpoints and the constant revision of them through a philosophical approach that involves critical reasoning in order for such standpoints to be challenged and become not a victim of scientific narrow mindedness and short-sightedness is fundamental. Finally, any research findings is a result of logical thinking. The research design here presented is based on the interpretive paradigm and the methodology which has been applied is the critical thinking. In addition to the reasons above stated, this choice was also because the author has had a profound interest in deepening his knowledge on philosophical research as well as he believes that knowledge emerges through active process and there is not a body of knowledge that holds the status of being exhaustive and that claims the absolute truth.

Fisher (2003) argues that critical thinking had its origins over 2000 years ago with its founder Socrates; however, the philosopher John Dewey is considered to be the father of the modern critical thinking approach.

> "…By defining critical thinking as an 'active' process, Dewey is contrasting it with the kind of thinking in which you just receive ideas and information from someone else – what you might reasonably call a 'passive' process. For Dewey, and for everyone who has worked in this tradition subsequently, critical thinking is essentially an 'active' process – one in which you think things through for yourself, raise questions yourself, find relevant information yourself, etc. rather than learning in a largely passive way from someone else". (Fisher, 2003 pp.2)

The critical thinking methodology was here applied using an iterative approach which involves the analysis of information through reflective, creative and critical reasoning in order for the generation of inferences and the drawing of conclusions (Horne & Wootton, 2005).

Chapter 3

Looking at Marketing from a Psychological Perspective

"It is not difficult to see why motivation has become one of the central areas of investigation for psychologists. The science of psychology is more than not defined as the study of behaviour and experience" (Evans, 1975 pp.9)

In order to better understand what triggers a person's behaviour an insight from within the psychology domain might be helpful. More specifically we seek information on motivation and the vectors that influence and define it.

In a concise way, there exist some elements such as a person's drives and instincts as well as their purposes and intentions that are inextricably related to and may determine human behaviour (Evan, 1975; Vernon, 1969). The drives and instincts are more associated with non-intentional behaviour, whereas the purposes and intentions are more related with intentional and purposive behaviour. In humans, purposes and intentions can be used to explain behaviour, more than drives and instincts, as these two last elements may not necessarily determine one's behaviour. Hence, the fact that a person is hungry does not mean that they will eat – consider, for example, a Christian who decides to avoid eating dinner for lent during Easter time. The purposes/intentions are in turn very much related to and influenced by incentives, goals and rewards; in other words, stimuli. Stimuli do have the potential to trigger classes of behaviour (Evans, 1975). Thus, they can be seen as the motives themselves for human behaviour. In addition, to stimulate behaviour other elements also play a part. They are the 'wants' and 'needs' of a person. So, considering what has been said so far, it is reasonable to say that motivation can take two forms: the intrinsic (e.g. wants and needs) and the extrinsic (incentives and rewards) (Reeve, 2005; Parkinson & Colman, 1995; Deci, 1976). In the case of Christians, it can be said that either forms of motivation may be deeply influenced by Christians' beliefs or, at least, moderated by them – hence, a person, who does not need a new pair of shoes, may want to buy a pair of shoes they find fashionable but feel refrained by their understanding of surplus or lack of consideration towards poor people who do not even have food to eat. However, the same person could justify the buying of an extra pair of shoes if they carried the label fair trade, since this would theoretically be helping poorer people. This nonetheless, does not discard the idea that a non-Christian would hold the same attitude and behaviour - perhaps for different reasons.

Another psychological aspect that may influence behaviour is emotion. Vernon (1969) suggests that emotional appraisal would appear to motivate action, however, it may not lead to action. This author affirms that some types of emotions may lead to behaviour; some not.

> "...Sympathy may be little more than a passive registration of the emotions of others, accompanied by corresponding emotions; whereas compassion stimulates us to take action to relieve the unhappiness of others. Yet all emotions enable us to evaluate objects and events, and judge their significance to us. They may even enable us to understand more fully than reason alone, especially in situations involving desires and actions of other people. Furthermore, they make possible the evaluation of our own actions, thus stimulating us to persist in certain courses of action which seem valuable to us, while desisting from others which are useless or harmful" (Vernon, 1969 pp.72).

The above statement has considerable importance for the understanding of the influence that emotions may have upon people's behaviour. It suggests that emotions are influenced by external stimuli and so that the social environment and elements pertaining to it like culture and sub-cultures (e.g. religion) may condition emotions (Pickton & Broderick, 2005; Belch & Belch, 2004; Steenkamp, 2001). Accordingly, Parrott (2001) points out that emotions have an effect on others, they are regulated by social roles and rules and modified by culture. For instance, Christians are taught to be compassionate towards people in need. Therefore, if the affirmation that compassion may lead a person to act (behave) in order to relieve other people's unhappiness or pain is true, it should be obvious that Christians would indeed be more likely to buy fair trade products or buy ethically, since the feeling of compassion would stimulate them to alleviate people's unhappiness caused by unfair commercial relations and practice. The statement that Christians are taught to be compassionate also implies that emotions can be learnt (e.g. experiential and vicarious learning (Pickton & Broderick, 2005)) and bolsters Parrott's (2001) idea that emotions can be influenced by external factors. In the same vein, Markus & Kitayama in Parrott (2001 pp.120) suggest that "a cultural groups way of feeling is shaped by the groups' habitual and normative social behaviour and, in turn, these ways of feeling influence the nature of this social behaviour". Consequently, one can say that emotions are in fact conditioned by environmental elements such as culture.

Yet, this argument still does not guarantee that some emotions will in practice lead to behaviour.

Vernon's suggestion about compassion implies that this emotion is an innate human condition. The author, however, does not agree with it, as otherwise poverty would not be an issue in today's society. Nonetheless, even considering that emotions such as compassion can be learnt or determined by social environment, crucial questions remain. Does learning to be compassionate lead to the feeling of compassion itself? Or is it a condition for this emotion to exist? Furthermore, the view that emotions can be learnt or conditioned and therefore may become part of a person's cluster of beliefs and attitude does not imply or mean that such beliefs and attitude will be translated into behaviour (Carrigan et al, 2004; Carrigan & Attallan, 2001; Shaw & Clarke, 1999; Yam-Tang & Chan, 1998). One could argue that being compassionate may purely be seen as a value dissociated from emotions which nonetheless may lead to a compassionate attitude and/or behaviour – hence, one may value life or social equity and yet feel comfortable with the idea of 'allies soldiers' killing to bring about 'justice'. In the case of Christians, learning to be compassionate may lead to the feeling of compassion. Nevertheless, the feeling of compassion does not necessarily lead to positive behaviour or any action whatsoever if other more 'tangible' elements do not trigger enough motivation to cause a personal state change. Therefore, the question whether Christians would in fact be more likely to buy fair-trade products is indeed pertinent, whether Christians' beliefs and attitudes and the emotions triggered by these beliefs and attitudes motivate Christians to engage in behaviour to alleviate other people's suffering and unhappiness.

Notwithstanding what has been said, a more comprehensive explanation about motivations and behaviour, one that considers psychological and social needs that may influence behaviour, is needed. Reeve (2005) highlights that needs cause people motivational states. In the case of psychological needs, the type of motivation that causes behaviour is intrinsic, people act in order to fulfil such needs that can derive from feelings of interest, freedom, competence and self-determination. The challenge of the activity is enough to motivate a person and it is an end in itself (Deci, 1976). Extrinsic motivation is associated with social needs and arises when the environment provides the stimuli, when it is known by a person that engaging in an activity may bring about positive or negative consequences. Thus, this type of motivation is dependent on external influences.

> "The essential difference between the two types of motivation lies in the source that energizes and directs the behaviour. With intrinsically motivated behaviour, the motivation emanates from psychological needs and spontaneous satisfaction the activity provides; with extrinsically motivated behaviour, the motivation emanates from incentives and consequences made contingent on the observed behaviour" (Reeve, 2005 pp.135).

Both types of needs could exert an influence on Christians' behaviour. Take the psychological needs such as feelings of self-determination or competence. A Christian could be motivated by these psychological needs when faced with the challenge of eradicating poverty or social injustice (which inevitably demands action) and in this way engage in action to solve these problems, since Christians would find self-determination in doing so through the influence of their faith – one needs to consider that faith is a different concept from beliefs. According to Christian teachings faith is a gift given by God that can be increased or taken away altogether depending on whether a person decides to live their life following Christianity's guidelines (e.g. The Ten Commandments) (Chapman, 1994). Take now the social needs perspective. Christians could engage in action to solve the poverty or social injustice problems because by doing so they give a testimony of their faith and receive social recognition and acceptance. Although, these affirmations could imply that Christians would this way find motivation to buy fair trade products (more than non-Christians) as a way of doing something about poverty or social injustice, this still does not guarantee that consumer behaviour would take place. For instance, agnostics may be motivated as much in the same fashion, however, with reasons determined by citizenship and strong feelings for self-realisation - in other words, they would be moved by their psychological needs of relatedness and social needs of achievement (Reeve, 2005). Moreover, a person (Christian or not) even if motivated to do something may become sceptical about its own capability to change a situation that overrides their power alone. That is, people could easily think that what they can do will change a given situation little or not at all and so prefer not to act whatsoever – this affirmation also implies that psychological and social (as intrinsic and extrinsic motives) needs can be repressed or ignored altogether, when the challenge faced seem to be beyond one's own strength.

Let us now consider that intrinsic motivation emerges mainly due to a psychological need that ought to be sufficed in order for a person to feel emotionally fulfilled. Given that extrinsic motivation is triggered by an environmental stimulus, it is then reasonable to say that due to a social need a person is motivated to act in order to suffice such a need, and consequently feel emotionally fulfilled. Reeve (2005), on his book entitled 'understanding motivation and emotion', classifies psychological and social needs as follows, respectively: needs of autonomy, competence and relatedness; needs of achievement, affiliation and intimacy and power. Some people will be more influenced by certain psychological and social needs than others or, better said, people have different levels of specific needs. The intensity of these needs will depend upon one's personality and it will be the personality of a person that will determine how they conceive the world and reality, how they feel and respond to an object or to a specific situation. Therefore, in order to have a better understanding about people's motivations to act it is necessary to understand the concept of personality through an overview of some theories on the subject.

Schiffman and Kanuk (1997 pp114) define personality as the "inner psychological characteristics that both determine and reflect how a person responds to his or her environment". These authors point out some personality theories such as the Freudian (the psychoanalytic theory of personality which is based on the stages of personality development: oral, anal, phallic, latency and genital stages); the Jungian (theory that highlights personality types such as the sensing-intuiting, thinking-feeling, extroversion-introversion and judging-perceiving); the Neo-Freudian theory (based on the influence that social relationships have on the development of personality - one example of such classification is the one proposed by Karen Horney which suggests three personality groups: compliant, aggressive and detached people) and the Trait theory which is defined as "...any distinguishing, relatively enduring way in which one individual differs from another" (Schiffman & Kanuk, 1997 pp125-126). From the above concept derive personality traits such as innovativeness, dogmatism, social character, optimum stimulation level, variety-novelty seeking, visualisers and verbalisers, need for cognition, fixated and compulsive consumption, and ethnocentrism. Similarly, Foxall et al (1998) point out that personality is related to an individual's characteristics that evokes consistent patterns of behaviour.

Foxall et al offer a more comprehensive classification for the personality concept. In addition to the above-mentioned personality groups/types these authors highlight Riesman's et al tradition-directed, inner-directed and other-directed classifications. Furthermore, Foxall et al (1998) suggest a deeper insight about personality based on concepts derived from the Jungian, Neo-Freudian and Traits theories. From this some classifications follow: extroverts (people who are sociable, need the company of others, active and impulsive) and introverts (people who are quiet, retiring and cautious), people who anxious, moody, easily depressed, over emotional or are calm, even-tempered, infrequent worriers, show temporary and slow emotional reactions (classification based on level of emotionality), people who are anti-social, insensitive to others, and even psychotic or people who are self-centred, independent, innovative and risk taking (classification based on level of tough-mindedness), people who are carried out by impulsiveness and venturesomeness (relates to level of sensation seeking). Finally, these authors offer a combined classification of personality that involves cognitive and personality traits. Based on the above varied classifications of personality, it would not be much of a presumption to affirm that relying on the fact that Christians would be more prone to buy fair trade products than anyone else because of their beliefs is to be ignoring many more elements that comprise and determine human behaviour, independently on their religious allegiance.

Mowen & Minor (1998) affirm that in order for personality to be defined four essential factors need to be considered: behaviour indicates consistency throughout time; this in turn will distinguish people from one another; behaviour is contextual; and a single measure of personality cannot foretell behaviour. Blythe (1997 pp39) highlights that personality "is the collection of individual characteristics that make a person unique, and which control an individual's responses to and relationship with the external environment". He goes onto offering some features of personality. It is integrated, self-serving, its characteristics are individualistic and unique, it is overt, and it is consistent. In addition, Blythe points out some theories regarding personality such as the psychoanalytic, typological, trait and factor and psychographics ones. Salomon (2002) defines personality as an individual's psychological 'makeup' and pinpoints that personality consistently influences how a person responds to their environment. This author also emphasises that recently new theories have emerged and point to the belief that actually persons' behaviour does not show consistent patterns and is dependent on different circumstances. That is, people seem not to have stable personalities.

The definition of personality is very much similar amongst various authors as well as its classifications remain around the same theories. One common aspect found amongst such definitions is the 'consistency of behaviour pattern' element, which implies that most of the people, because of their personalities, show a somewhat consistent behaviour - despite the fact that depending on circumstances people's behaviour may indicate some variance. Moreover, it is plausible to say that although personality is unique to every person, there are elements that are commonly shared amongst various people (be it within a specific socio-cultural context (e.g. nationally) or even across different socio-cultural contexts (internationally)). It is exactly based on these factors that tactics such as segmentation through psychographics have been widely applied within the marketing domain (Pickton & Broderick, 2005; Belch and Belch, 2004;

Jobber, 2004; Czinkota & Ronkainen, 2004; Stokes, 2003; Kotler, 2003; Salomon, 2002; Foxal et al, 1998; Schiffman & Kanuk, 1997; Blythe, 1997; Hofstede, 1981).

However, even considering the point that people share some personality traits/characteristics and therefore can be allocated into psychographics groups, this still cannot be taken as a premise to predict behaviour. The author believes in the behaviourist approach (Shaffer, 2002) of seeing behaviour and that in fact behaviour can change according to the influence of environmental stimuli. So even people who share similar traits may nonetheless show different reactions when facing the same situation - hence, people who are extremely sociable but come from a different socio-economic background may behave very differently when going to a party. Moreover (related to the study here proposed), just because people consider themselves Christian it does not imply that they will share similar personalities, nor does it mean (contrary to common sense) that they will share similar personality traits that will trigger the need to help other people through an action – hence, although the Christian teachings are the same for all, everyone, for one reason, because of their personalities and their unique way to respond to the environment, will interpret the same teachings in a different way. For one person to love the neighbour may mean to pray for them, whereas for another, it may actually mean to buy a fair-trade product. In addition, the interpretation of the same message will also be influenced by the way individuals evaluate the world and what is around them, and this in turn is what determines people's attitude.

Salomon (2002 pp198) highlights that "...an attitude is a lasting, general evaluation of people (including oneself), objects, advertisements, or issues". Based on this argument it is possible to say that attitude and beliefs are very much symbiotic terms and also, that at no time it implies that behaviour derives from it. According to Krech & Crutchfield (1928) cited by Kiesler et al (1969), attitude is the intensity of a positive or a negative individual's affection towards or against a psychological object with the latter being described as any symbol, person, phrase or idea. Taking into consideration this definition, it is reasonable to affirm that it will depend on the level of positive affection towards Christian teachings and beliefs that a person will develop a Christian attitude to life and their evaluations about events, people and issues will be biased by it. In addition, based on Christian teachings (it is very clear on the Catechism book of the Catholic Church when it talks about the Ten Commandments) there is no way to be considered a Christian if such beliefs and attitude in essence are not based on concrete actions, as otherwise this would contradict the very example of Jesus Christ. Thus, it seems that holding such an attitude would compel a Christian to act, even if one could still not guarantee it. However, it would not necessarily mean the buying of a product to further help other people – a Christian could simply think that better than just buying a fair-trade product is to actually go to Africa and work amongst those in need. In addition, free-will (Chapman, 1994) is another concept in Christianity that is much respected and emphasized. Yet, one could still argue that in many societies Christian teachings have emphasized the concept of sin and hell as its consequence. Therefore, Christians fearing such consequences would feel compelled to do the good, at least as a way to redeem their mistakes (sins) against their religion. This in turn could be used by marketers as a premise to justify their belief on Christian 'willingness' to buy fair trade products – this is an interesting argument, however, there is nothing in the Christian teachings indicating that not buying fair trade products is a sin which goes against social justice, people's neighbours or even God. Furthermore, buying a fair-trade product that is superfluous to a person could well (though for many distortedly) be seen as a sin of selfishness and therefore, it would be a condemned act in itself.

As far as can be seen to this point, it is not possible, from only a psychological perspective, to conclude that Christians are more likely than non-Christians to buy fair trade products. The psychological theories explored above not only spur on the aim of the research, but may contain answers to new questions yet to emerge as we explore from a new perspective. The next section will look at marketing from an ethical perspective.

Chapter 4

Looking at Marketing from an Ethical Perspective

The previous chapter explored aspects of human psychology with the intention of understanding whether elements such as emotion, personality and attitude would offer a basis for the determination of, or at least, what triggered peoples' motivations when taking a buying decision. The non-exhaustive conclusion was that these psychological aspects do have an impact on human beings' motivation (be them Christians or not). However, theories of motivation may not be used to predict a specific behaviour other than in a probabilistic sense – by the inference from identified but unmet needs. Identification of general consumer needs is helpfully informative, but the extent of the need can only be known at the level of the individual, as can the all-important extent to which an identified need is already met from sources other than purchasing particular goods and services. The author will now explore the original and the newly emerging issues from an ethical perspective.

According to Green (1994), ethics and morality terms have been used within literature with interchangeable meanings to describe, explain or systematically study values through which people hold their judgements about right and wrong behaviour. He pinpoints that from an etymological perspective the words ethics and morality hold similar meanings and this justifies the interchangeable use of them to refer to the same subject without more specific distinctions – just because language terms share etymological communalities, it does not mean that they need to be treated as the same. Perhaps it is actually because of such looseness of terms that ethics becomes a confusing and paradoxical discipline. Beauchamp & Bowie (2004 pp1), on the other hand, do make a distinction between morality and ethical theory, affirming that "morality is concerned with the social practices defining right and wrong. The practices – together with other kinds of customs, rules, and mores – are transmitted within cultures and institutions from generation to generation. Similar to political constitution and natural languages, morality exists prior to the acceptance (or rejection) of its standards by particular individuals" – this is an interesting standpoint, but one that imposes a concept of morality and implies that people are passive to it, that people are not able to reject the moral practices existent in one determined culture. The author does not believe in such argument, since one of the characteristics of famous Christian martyrs was to actually live in a way that challenged the concepts of morality of their epoch and even to introduce new conceptions of them (e.g. Moses and the Ten Commandments). Beauchamp & Bowie go onto explain that "the terms ethical theory and moral philosophy point to the reflection on the nature and justification of right actions".

Beauchamp & Bowie's viewpoint about morality shares common ground with Aristotle's concept of moral knowledge which claims that it can only be acquired through practical experience and habit. Norman (1998) interprets this acquisition of moral knowledge as a consequence of moral education, which is translated into being told in various situations what appropriate behaviour would be suitable for such occasions. In this way, a person would achieve an intuitive sense that will shape their behaviour and direct them to act according to it – it seems that there is a convincing truth in such an argument, since social research has shown repeatedly that social behaviour may be influenced (positively or negatively) by parental rearing and behaviour models such as celebrities, during a person's childhood and adolescence (Rosenkoetter et al, 2004; Boxer & Tisak, 2003; Persegani et al, 2001; Low & Durkin, 2001).

.

> "The problem whether morality can be taught is not a new one. Plato grappled with it in his dialogues *Meno* and *Protagoras,* and faced the difficulty of saying what virtue is, let alone whether it is possible to teach it. Yet it may well seem surprising that so many difficulties can be raised. Do not most of us hold some set of moral principles, even if not very reflectively? Is it not common to engage in moral debate, with the hope of getting closer to the truth? Furthermore, most people do not see moral awareness as an optional extra, a minor accomplishment alongside others." (Benn, 1998 pp2).

Even considering both possibilities, that morality can and cannot be taught or acquired, this theoretical impasse only adds to the complexity of dilemmas such as what is morally right or wrong. Or questions like: even taking into consideration the possibility that a group of people may hold similar moral values, does this fact refrain some of them to make decisions which go against the common sense belief of the group? Does it protect them from other external influences when they are dispersed in other social groups that do not share their moral values? Yet, does it mean one becomes unresponsive to his own reasoning and questionings about what is right or wrong?

The points of view of the authors above are nonetheless very relevant, for they imply that moral judgement, or knowing what is morally right or wrong, can actually be determined by one's upbringing - perhaps, to a good extent, passively or even unconsciously. This has implications to Christians' motivations and behaviour, since according to such logic behaviour would be shaped by a person's understanding about what is right or wrong in the light of what would be imparted to them through their Christian education. As already known, Christianity preaches that one should be compassionate, caring and strive for justice. Thus, being or by doing so would indicate what is for Christians morally right. Illustratively, this in turn could be translated into buying a fair-trade product, because morally speaking it would be the right thing to do, since fair trade products are meant to promote social justice.

Yet, such simplicity of thought cannot be taken as a premise for prediction of behaviour, as it is also known that one thing is to learn what is right and wrong morally, the other is to comply with these beliefs. Moreover, human beings are by nature cynical towards any sort of information that is imposed by parents or institutions without any reasonable or understandable justification for them – how many times throughout our growing and maturing process did we ask our teachers, an adult or our parents why we should do this or that and the answer we have received was: because I say so! Or, this is the right way to behave! And what did such answers trigger in us? Benn (1998 pp2) touches this and previous questions here stated and bolster the existence of such dilemmas when talking about moral authority and proposing that "…we might still be disturbed by the suggestion that some individuals, traditions or institutions, are moral authorities. We might think that individuals should be left to make up their own minds about what is right and wrong, that they should not be indoctrinated and should certainly not be coerced". Such affirmation encompasses all people with no exception. There is no evidence that Christians would not be affected by this way of thinking, yet there is also no evidence that they would. Furthermore, everyone (Christian or non-Christian) is constantly bombarded by new ideas and beliefs imposed by the environment or by someone like an actor or singer they highly esteem or admire – a person may admire a celebrity for their professional success and self-determination, even though such 'models' might not be morally admirable. Nonetheless, the world is full of examples of people that perhaps even unconsciously want to look and behave like those very same celebrities and even accept these individuals' worldview as their own. Perhaps, with a deeper insight within ethics and some of its well-known theories one can find a solid premise to ascertain whether Christians would be more inclined/likely to act ethically (right or wrong…it is still be found out) through, say, the buying of fair-trade products.

It is a common definition amongst authors that ethical or moral judgement is normative and indicates how an individual should or should not act in the face of a morally questionable situation. This is often seen as the 'ought to' and 'ought not to' thoughts or action-guiding "ought" (Beauchamp & Bowie, 2004; Sterba, 1998; Green,1994). Norman (1998) points out that the question about how to act cannot be answered through appealing to established norms and that it is indispensable to confront the question about why one should act one a way rather than another - in a nutshell, the reasons for behaviour. Green (1994) distinguishes ethics from other normative instances like prudence, etiquette and law – although one could question whether laws, prudence or etiquette are a result of ethical norms within a society or ethical norms are a consequence of the influence of those elements. Either way, they seem not to be very easily distinguishable as Green suggests. He also affirms that in order to have a 'complete approach to ethics' one needs to be able to answer three different questions: the one of value (which values are relevant for or which we want to promote); the one of virtue or moral character (what makes one good or bad); and the one of right conduct (the need to know what is right and what is wrong in order to assess a situation and act morally right) – this last question being the more relevant to ethics, and again the argument implies that morality is learnt. Green separates what he calls 'less-than-adequate-views' (egoism, relativism, right as religious traditions and right as conscience alone) about ethics from the ones he considers to be proper theories derived from deontological (duty) and teleological (goals) approaches to ethics – a rather confusing separation, since religion has been the basis for many ethical theories such as the Kantian (Kant himself was a Christian before becoming a Philosopher). Also, the suggestion that there exist less-than-adequate ethical views or theories implies an imposition of ethical truths, and this in itself is questionable.

According to Norman (1998), Plato's and Aristotle's main concern is to present a 'good and virtuous way of life' as the one which gives an individual reason to follow it, as by doing so will provide them with the happiest and most fulfilling states in life. This way of reasoning can be associated with the concept of egoism in ethical language, given that the main concern here is to act morally not for the sake of the moral act itself, but because acting morally will bring about positive consequences for a person, no matter what a person's conception of happiness may be – controversially, what would a drug addict think about fulfilling state? Green (1994 pp57) suggests that "Ethical egoism is the view that holds that an act is right when it best promotes the individual's long-term self-interest". Interestingly, this concept has a quasi 'subtle' connection with the psychological concept of extrinsic motivation (seen in the previous section), which claims that a person finds motivation to engage in an activity because it is aware that such an activity will be the means to achieve the final goal; the reward. Norman also highlights that in counter position to Plato's and Aristotle's ideas, H.A. Prichard (1928), on his lecture entitled 'Duty and Interest', affirmed that justice done because it is advantageous for an individual cannot be claimed to be justice. Here, the promotion of justice is simply an act of self-interest. Whereas, the just person is someone who acts justly simply because doing otherwise would go against the very same principle of justice. Prichard's viewpoint is very similar to Kant's concept of duty (which consists of complying with one's duty for its own sake), which is also related to the concept of altruism (Norman, 1998). Again, such concepts find a relation with the psychological perspective about intrinsic motivation, which claims that an individual engages in an activity motivated by the activity itself. Based on what has been said, even considering that Christian teachings proactively emphasise justice or love towards other people, from a moral perspective, Christians can nonetheless fall into both categories: the egoistic and the altruistic. This in turn does not signify that they may not act morally right, independently of which perspective is taken into consideration, even if they do not buy fair trade products. However, it does also not indicate that even if promoting justice is seen as morally wrong a Christian will not necessarily choose to promote it. Be it self-interest or be it feelings of duty what motivates a person to act, these may not necessarily be translated into the buying of fair-trade products. Since one may justify not buying such products because they argue not be able to see what benefits they are causing to others (hence, causing benefits to others is here one of the conditions to feel happy) or to himself (as they have to pay more to buy fair trade goods and still may not be satisfied with their quality) – not buying fair trade products would be in this case morally right. The same justification could be taken using the altruistic perspective - if one has not enough tangible information about what fair trade products are all about, who guarantees that buying them will promote any justice or other peoples' happiness? And even if they had access to enough information, is buying fair trade products really a duty? This leads to the belief that perhaps moral judgement or the concept of right and wrong is purely relative.

Beauchamp & Bowie (2004 pp7-8) describe relativism as a descriptive claim to morality. They highlight that "…In the early part of the twentieth century, defenders of relativism used discoveries of anthropologists in the South Sea Islands, Africa, and South America as evidence of a diversity of moral practices throughout the world. Their empirical discoveries about what is the case led them to the conclusion that rightness is contingent on cultural beliefs and that the concepts of rightness and wrongness are meaningless apart from the specific contexts in which they arise". Thus, a moral belief found in one society cannot be expected to be found in another, and therefore it can be assumed that what is morally right for one society is not necessarily right for another. Although relativists claim that there is no absolute or universal truth about the understanding of moral values, they end up being a victim of their own relativism, as tolerance in this instance, ironically, becomes a universal value (Green, 1994). Nonetheless, if the relativist argument is correct, it implies that beyond cultural boundaries moral norms, values and behaviour are indeed relative. This also implies that the environment in which a person is brought up has a major impact on their understanding about right and wrong doing. Because it is known that people within a culture can be further subdivided into sub-cultures or "tribes" and influenced by their norms of conduct (Cova & Cova, 2002; Steemkamp, 2001), this leads to the belief that Christians' concept of morality are indeed shaped by Christian teachings/community life's influence. However - and here comes the persistent controversial point – does knowing, been taught and/or influenced by a cultural concept of what is right and wrong provided by Christian institutions or parenthood mean that a person will unconditionally choose the morally right doing? As much as it may be uncomfortable to the author, there exist examples of scandals in abundance about anti-social behaviour (in a more polite way of putting it) by priests and other people who have been held as moral models for centuries or at least were. From this angle, not even the claim that the understanding of morality is relative to the cultural context can be upheld anymore, unless the concept of cultural context has been eradicated from or radically modified in today's society - Globalisation may be the major responsible for such. For instance, Cova & Cova, (2002) suggest the idea of tribalisation of post-modern society and that people gather together or choose different tribes to join in, becoming part of them through shared links and motives. Undoubtedly, based on Cova & Cova's perspective, one could say that cultural context is taken to a different level of understanding, since tribes are not constrained to territorial or cultural boundaries. They are the emergence of new culture – examples abound in today's society: 'Capoeiristas' (people who train and hold Capoeira (a Brazilian martial art spread around the world)) as a philosophy of life; Harley Davison's devotees (tribes) around the world, surfers, skate boarders, Manchester United fans and so forth. Intriguingly, even before the 'tribalisation' of post-modern society concept existed, Christian 'tribes' have already been around as well as their understanding of moral values and judgment overcome cultural boundaries for thousands of years. In summary, not only the concept of cultural context by now cab be taken as relative, but also the concept of relativism is in itself relative, since Christian parameters of morality is the same everywhere in the world – what may happen is that people bend these parameters to allow themselves to act immorally. Finally, even believing that Christians from different cultures would hold relative concepts of what is right or wrong, yet it offers little help to judge whether the buying of fair trade goods is morally right or wrong nor does it explain or justify the reasons for one's consumer behaviour towards fair-trade goods, let alone to predict behaviour.

Another way of describing morality is through seeing 'right as conscience alone' (Green, 1994). According to this viewpoint, one would come to know what is right or wrong purely by the influence of their own conscience. Although this theory implies that conscience is a unique trait to every person, it is nonetheless self-evident that it lacks of solid foundations, as conscience is presented as an autonomous entity that directs and determines moral behaviour. This theory also suffers the absence of consideration of the social influence on people's behaviour. The author suggests that the term 'conscience' in this case is misplaced by or mistaken from the concept of 'intuitive thought' which is primarily a stage of human cognitive development and is virtually achieved by trial and error (Piaget,

2001). Thus, from this perspective the only way to achieve moral judgment or the understanding of right and wrong would be through repetitive 'judgment trials' in order to reach a level where a person would develop 'moral schemas', which in turn would shape their moral beliefs and behaviour. Nevertheless, ironically, such way of seeing moral conscience denies the very concept of conscience as a 'ready-only' one and emphasizes it as being shaped by the influence of external stimuli or environment – hence, life is not like a theatrical play where social interference can somewhat be controlled. However, even if one was to use this perspective to understand or bolster the prediction of human motives and behaviour, that would still lead to the conclusion that, using the words of Green (1994 pp65), "what my conscience tells me" is something accessible only to me and no one else, and therefore it is not possible to foretell whether a person would see, say, the buying of fair trade products as morally right or wrong; independently whether a person is a Christian. In addition, how would the knowing of one person's belief that fair-trade products are morally right make any difference for marketers? And since everyone has different ways of perceive reality, would it mean that a significant number of people share the belief that fair trade is morally right? If so, does it mean they all would buy it?

Moreover, hence that fair-trade products are a relatively newness and that it would take a few 'judgment trials' in order for a person to morally 'calibre' their conscience, which even though would still lead to two options: the buying of fair-trade products are morally right, or not. Furthermore, considering that they are morally right, the argument goes back to the question whether this guarantees that a Christian or a non-Christian will buy them.

One of the most influential theories from the teleological perspective is the utilitarianism (Beauchamp & Bowie, 2004; Shaw, 1999; Benn, 1998; Norman, 1998; Green, 1994). According to Shaw (1999 pp2) "Two fundamental ideas underlie utilitarianism: first, that the results of our actions are the key to their moral evaluation, and second, that one should assess and compare those results in terms of the happiness or unhappiness they cause (or, more broadly, in terms of their impact on people's well-being)". Beauchamp & Bowie (2004 pp17) pinpoint that, in the light of utilitarian viewpoint, "An action or practice is right if it leads to the best possible balance of good consequences over bad consequences for all the parties affected". Green (1994) emphasises that the 'utilitarians' admit that all human beings search for happiness and that happiness is connoted as being the ultimate satisfaction of one's most important desires. Yet, the same author says that according to utilitarian theory, an action is morally judged as right if it promotes 'the greatest amount of happiness for the greatest number of people'. From such affirmation conflicts arise. Is it possible to reach a point where everyone understands one another to the extent that they know what is best for each other without being biased by their own interests and 'most important desires'? Or, is it possible for them to reach a consensus about what happiness mean? It is enough to know that approx. 6 billion people (7 Billion nowadays) make up the whole global population and that an enterprise such as this would at least (being optimistic) demand an individual selfless time-consuming effort, and facts from the actual global society do not point to this belief. Moreover, what does 'most important desires' mean to every single living person? How does one define happiness/unhappiness? And who is to hold the truth about the concept of happiness/unhappiness? In addition to such questions, if there are not absolute answers to them, how can an action be morally judged universally as right or wrong?

Applying the Christian/fair trade example associated with an utilitarian assessment of morality, in one hand one could affirm that the buying of fair-trade products would indeed help to promote the greatest happiness to the greatest number of people, since the majority of global population live below the poverty line – 4billion people live in poverty (Czinkota & Ronkainen, 2004); more than 30.000 people are killed by poverty every single day (Newconsumer, 2004); and 80 per cent of the world's income belong to the richest 20 per cent of the world's population (CAFOD, Christian Aid, SCIAF, 2004). On the other hand, based on these and on the following examples one also wonders whether the concept of 'greatest happiness' to the 'greatest number of people' is sensibly understood - unfair trade costs the developing countries US$ 700 billion a year and in 1999 the global military expenditure amounted more than US$ 700billion (CAFOD, Christian Aid and SCIAF, 2004) – in 2019 the expenditure with military was 1,73 US$ Trillion. Yet, to cancel the debts of the 53 most affected countries it would be necessary to spend only three times the amount of money the British spend on Hula Hoops, a staggering £300 billion! War is the major cause of poverty and Europe spends a staggering £7.5billion a year on ice-cream alone (CAFOD, Christian Aid and SCIAF, 2004) – of course the actual figures a much higher.

Some people would simply argue that the buying of fair-trade products can promote very little happiness to very few people (since these products are mainly marketed to the population (which has to pay more) of developed countries such as USA and EU countries, which by far outweighs the number of people benefited by fair-trade initiative – e.g. only 120.000 producers have benefited from UK expenditure on fair trade products (CAFOD, Christian Aid & SCIAF, 2004). In addition, the 'greatest happiness' for those benefited people cannot be reduced to fair wages anyway. Furthermore, would anyone from westernised cultures which are known for their individualistic, materialistic, hedonistic and consumerist traits (Sun et al, 2004; O'Shaughnessy & O'Shaughnessy, 2002) care about others' greatest happiness? Finally, would not the promotion of fair-trade products be ethically wrong, since it stimulates consumption and this according to O'Shaughnessy & O'Shaughnessy (2002 pp528) "is the most tangible expression of attempts at marketing-directed hedonism"? In the end therefore, from the utilitarian perspective, the buying of fair-trade products could even be seen as morally wrong. If so, using a utilitarian moral point of view to understand the motives of or predict Christians' and non-Christians' behaviour alike towards buying fair trade products would be misleading at the least, since it would be morally wrong for them to buy such products, yet some still buy them. Therefore, the utilitarian moral standpoint cannot be used to understand Christians' or anyone else's motives and behaviour, let alone to help predict the latter.

To add to the complexity, the problem is that Christian moral beliefs are not based on utilitarianism but on a concept much closer to the Feminist Ethics or Ethics of Care (Beauchamp & Bowie, 2004); yet not quite. "Feminist philosophers have pointed out that traditional theories present a conception of morality that leaves little room for virtues such as empathy, compassion, fidelity, love and friendship. An understanding of the context of a situation is particularly important when taking into account the distinctive "voice" that many psychologists, philosophers and management theorists have associated with women" (Beauchamp & Bowie, 2004 pp34). The feminist instance is concerned with relationships, in particular, to the needs and their well-being of others (Beauchamp & Bowie, 2004; Sterba, 1998) - the whole feminist moral concept is curiously very much similar to Mary's (the mother of Jesus) example of life, and since Mary's example has been imparted throughout the last 2000 years by the Catholic Church, one wonders whether the very feminist approach is just not a modern version of what has existed for centuries already. One way or the other, as highlighted in chapter 3, the understanding or learning of 'virtues' such as compassion or love still does not indicate or guarantees that Christians will buy fair trade products, although it could be seen, from a feminist or Marian standpoint, as morally right. Nonetheless, one still cannot guarantee that Christians or whoever takes the feminist paradigm as theirs (even if considering being caring, loving, compassionate and so forth, morally right) will at all classify buying such products within their understanding of such 'virtues' – for many being loving may mean being polite; being caring may mean not being irresponsible and being compassionate may mean to have mercy.

In reality, if at all, Christians should be much more influenced by the morality concept derived from the natural law, a theory developed by Thomas Aquinas (who is considered a Saint in Catholic Church) that according to Singer (1994) is the premise on which the Catholic Church built up its "semi-official" philosophy. In a more modest though more precise statement, Cahn & Markie (1998) present Thomas Aquinas as the developer of a synthesis of Aristotelian and Christian doctrine. John Locke in Singer (1994 pp249) highlights that "The state of nature has a law of nature to govern it, which obliges every one, and reason, which is that law, teaches all mankind, who will but consult it, that being all equal and independent, no one ought to harm another in his life, health, liberty or possessions..." – since equality is not a trait of the actual society, harming one's life, health, liberty or possessions could be seen as morally justifiable by the natural law concept (Iraq's war is a good example of it) - what is to be said about not buying fair trade products? Although John Locke's statement is somewhat congruent with what can be found in the Roman Catholic Catechism (Chapman, 1994), the concept of Christian morality derives much more from the teachings (e.g. Ten Commandments, Sermon of the Mount and so forth) of Christ, Who Christians (as the author) believe to be God Himself. This in turn does not make ethical/moral matters easier to understand or simpler to discern; let alone to put into practice in today's society. Below the excerpts from Mathew's Gospel (5:38-48) and John (13:34) respectively, slightly highlight the complexity and comprehensiveness of Christian ethics.

38 "You have heard that it was said, 'An eye for an eye and a tooth for a tooth''.

39 "But I tell you not to resist an evil person. But whoever slaps you on your right cheek, turn the other to him also".
40 "If anyone wants to sue you and take away your tunic, let him have your cloak also."
41 "And whoever compels you to go one mile, go with him two".
42 "Give to him who asks you, and from him who wants to borrow from you do not turn away".
43 "You have heard that it was said, 'You shall love your neighbour and hate your enemy.'
44 "But I say to you, love your enemies, bless those who curse you, do good to those who hate you, and pray for those who spitefully use you and persecute you",
45 "That you may be sons of your Father in heaven; for He makes His sun rise on the evil and sends rain on the just and the unjust"
46 "For if you love those who love you, what reward have you? Do not even the tax collectors do the same?"
47 "And if you greet your brethren only, what do you do more than others? Do not even the tax collectors do so?"
48 "Therefore you shall be perfect, just as your Father in heaven is perfect".

"Jesus said to his disciples: 'Love your neighbour even as I have loved you'".

Based on the above excerpt, especially verse 41 and 42, one could affirm that Christians ought to buy fair trade products in order to act morally right, given that to follow Christ's teachings is a condition to be become a Christian. However, the buying of a fair trade good may not be seen as an act of pure giving, as in this case one receives something in return. Therefore, that could actually be seen as an act biased by self-interest/individualism/materialism/hedonism/egoism. This in turn goes against the very Christian concept of love, which not only frees people from any conditioning, but also very often requires sacrifice (Chatel, 2003). Thus, the buying of fair-trade products (depending on the intention of the buyer and the meaning they give to such action) can be morally wrong for Christians. However, whether one is Christian or not, they still expect product quality, availability, reasonable price and convincing information. These expectations seem to be much more related to convenience and self-benefit than sacrifice and love for others. In addition, one could argue that given the fact that for-profit organisations are the ones 'asking' or, perhaps, manipulating a person's feelings of goodness and helpfulness with the excuse to further help poor producers, could the buying of fair-trade goods be seen as morally right? One could argue why these same companies do not take the initiative themselves to invest a small percentage of their profit margins to pay fairer wages, which they should be doing anyway.

The biggest challenge for ethics in determining what is morally right or wrong, is to reach understanding about what constitutes other people's interests and well-being as well as consensus about the relative compelling concerns of compassion, love and care, i.e. about the very concept of morally right or wrong. One starts to wonder, based on any moral standpoint (even the egoistic one), whether most people actually think, or let alone, act morally. Thus, there seems no ethical perspective that can help to support the idea of Christians' (or any person's) propensity or likelihood to buy fair-trade products, let alone helping marketers to predict consumer behaviour. Moreover, the buying of fair-trade products can, from various ethical perspectives, be held to be morally wrong. In any event, is knowing any of this of any practical use to marketers? Christians' and non-Christians' consumer motives and behaviour seem to be dependent on factors other than ethics or morality. Perhaps looking at marketing from a biological perspective may prove more helpful. To this we now turn in the next step of our critical exploration.

Chapter 5

Looking at Marketing from a Biological Perspective

As mentioned in chapter 3, from a psychological standpoint it is hard to establish a coherent and comprehensive argument which bolsters the idea that a Christian would probably hold a positive attitude towards fair trade products, let alone allow that attitude to influence his or her behaviour as a consumer. The terrain from an ethical perspective was similarly blurred. Ethical theories about moral behaviour seemed only to describe what morality is and to point to vague guidelines for moral action. In this chapter, the author will explore perspectives related to human biological traits, more specifically, to theories of genetic inheritance.

It is necessary to make it clear that the author does not base this chapter on the concept of biological determinism which suggests that "...all human behaviour

– hence all human society – is governed by a chain of determinants that runs from the gene to the individual to the sum of the behaviours of all individuals. The determinists would have it, then, that human nature is fixed by our genes" (Rose et al, 1985 pp6)". Biological determinists believe that social disparities in status, power and wealth in contemporary industrialised societies are biologically determined and therefore unchangeable. Such argument suffers its own weakness, as, if accepted as there would be few explanations for the rise and fall of the Soviet Union, or for the concept of human rights. One could argue that many Indians, for example, are conditioned by their caste system and this is the main reason for their non-economical ascension rather than any genetically limited potential to improve their social status and wealth. The argument about biologically determined behaviours and social reality finds its contradictions amongst even defenders of biological determinism. For instance, three authors from the Harvard University in their book entitled 'the role of brain disease in riots and urban violence' suggest that the behaviour of urban rioters is determined by brain dysfunction, since only a small group of people within a nation engage in arson, sniping, and physical assault and the majority do not. But then they affirm that environmental conditions, if wrong at the 'important time', can result in anatomical maldevelopment of their brain and that this is not reversible (Rose et al, 1985). The problem here is not only that these authors base their argument on the fact that electroencephalographic abnormalities have been found in the temporal region of the brain with much greater frequency in people who show violent and assaultive behaviour, than in people who show normal brain patterns. However, it may be argued that such abnormalities may have been caused by a change in the patients' emotional state when undergoing examinations. There is a whole range of chemical reactions that may cause alterations in electrographic machines' results and emotions cause (or are caused by?) changes in chemical states. It has been suggested that people at some 'important time' (whose concept is not explained) have their behaviour conditioned (their brain malformed?) forever (by what environmental influences?) These tautological loops are at best unhelpful, at worst *reductio ad absurdum*. Environmental influence *per se* cannot modify a persons' anatomic morphology unless through major accidents. Furthermore, if social misbehaviour is to be usefully viewed as a consequence of brain biological dysfunction, is assaultive behaviour or violence to be excused on medical grounds? Potentially all of us are capable of engaging in violent behaviour, especially with the influence of external stimuli such as TV programmes and films that instigate violent behaviour (Rosenkoetter et al, 2004; Boxer & Tisak, 2003; Low & Durkin, 2001; Persegani et al, 2001; Raviv et al, 1999). Finally, such theory ought to be viewed with some scepticism since its emergence was related to political manoeuvres to decrease urban violence in the US during the 1980's. Biological determinists such as Richard Dawkins (who claims that science is immune from political influence) are themselves not immune from political and social influences. What are we to conclude from the fact that Hitler and Mussolini shared their ideas?

Biology here will only be used as one means to better understand the whole concept of human behaviour in general and hence consumer behaviour in particular. In 'A Short History of Nearly Everything', written by the well-known author Bill Bryson (2004 pp.482), there is a precise description of DNA (some understanding of the nature of DNA is needed here, since it is germane to what will be considered next).

> "We are also uncannily alike. Compare your genes with any other human being's and on average they will be about 99.9 per cent the same. That is what makes us a species. The tiny difference in that remaining 0.1 per cent – 'roughly one nucleotide base in every thousand', to quote

the British geneticist and recent Nobel laureate John Sulston – are what endow us with our individuality...every human genome is different. Otherwise we would be identical. It is the endless recombinations of our genomes – each nearly identical to all the others, but not quite – that make us what we are, both individuals and a species.

But what exactly is this thing we call genome? And what, come to that, are genes?...Inside the cell is a nucleus and inside each nucleus are the chromosomes – forty-six little bundles of complexity, of which twenty-three come from your mother and twenty-three from your father. With a very few exceptions, every cell in your body – 99.999 per cent of them, say – carries the same complement of chromosomes. Chromosomes constitute the complete set of instructions necessary to make and maintain you and are made of long strands of the little wonder chemical called deoxyribonucleic acid or DNA – 'the most extraordinary molecule on Earth', as it has been called.

DNA exists for just one reason – to create more DNA – and you have a lot of it inside you: nearly 2 metres of it squeezed into almost every cell. Each length of DNA comprises some 3.2billion letters of coding, enough to provide "3,480,000,000 x 10" possible combinations, 'guaranteed to be unique against all conceivable odds', in the words of Christian de Duve...a one followed by more than three billion zeros. 'It would take more than five thousand average-size books just to print that figure', notes de Duve."

Within the literature the concepts about DNA and genes vary slightly with descriptions of chromosomes (e.g. its total numbers in humans are 23 pairs = 46) being very much the same (Davies, 2001; Brownie & Kernohan, 1999; Blackstock, 1998; Mader, 1995). However, on the whole their descriptions are very similar to the above-mentioned quote. Brownie & Kernohan (1999) affirm that DNA is the element of chromosomes that contains genetic information. Blackstock (1998) says that chromosomes are the result of the union of 'minibands' which in turn are loaded with DNA. Mader (1995) points out that during human reproduction each parent contributes with 23 chromosomes. In a more simplistic way, a new born human is indeed made up of half of each parents' genetic material, they are literally the resulting combination of two human beings. It would be possible therefore to speculate that understanding how parents are and behave there would be a considerable likeability to understand how the new born person would act in the future. Nonetheless, considering the above information about the possible genetic combinations in humans and also environmental elements that influence behaviour (Reeve, 2005; DiLalla, 2004; Shaffer, 2003; Carson & Rothstein, 1999), it seems that such an endeavour would not lead to much success. Moreover, there still is uncertainty about whether behaviour is pre-determined by one's genes or whether it is purely a result of environmental influence. Or, if it is a combination of the two, to what extent each element influences behaviour. Mader (1995) pinpoints that there have been attempts to answer this very question through studies involving twins. "It has been found that fraternal twins even when raised in the same environment are not remarkably similar in behaviour, whereas identical twins [derived from a single fertilized egg] raised separately are sometimes remarkably similar" (Mader, 1995 pp371). DiLalla (2004) as well as Carson & Rothstein (1999) mention studies involving twins to compare similarities in their behavioural traits and shared genetic influence. DiLalla affirms that researchers have found that 'disinhibitory personality traits' such as aggression and harm avoidance are mediated by genetic factors, and correlations between personality traits (e.g. social deviance and excitement seeking) and alcohol problems.

Although such studies show intriguing results and could be used by marketers in the future to understand consumer behaviour, some considerations need to be made. Firstly, only identical twins show very similar behaviour patterns; however, even this finding is not a certainty in all cases. Nonetheless, one could affirm that since twins share exactly at the same time the same genetic material from their parents, this explains their close similarity in behaviour. Interestingly, any other child from the same parents would also receive the same genetic material from both of them, and yet they are born unique and their behaviours take different forms. From this, it is plausible to conclude that either identical twins receive half of the half of their parents' chromosomes (11.5 chromosomes from each parent), which biologically is not possible or is yet to be discovered to be so. Or, each spermatozoid and egg bear themselves a unique combination of genetic information that will influence one's (or 'two's') behaviour in a unique fashion. Secondly, unless marketers treat everyone as twins (and still there would be millions of pairs of twins presenting different behaviour patterns), such knowledge has little relevance for marketing, given that nonetheless 'uniqueness' seems to be one of the most relevant traits of humans. It is necessary to consider that these researches are very much based on statistical analysis and therefore may be missing social aspects that cannot be measured mathematically and yet that have a determining influence on human behaviour. Although Carson & Rothstein (1999) believe that twins and adoption studies are needed in order to 'disentangle' environmental from genetic influences and to estimate the extent of each of these influences, the author, as argued previously, faces such belief with much scepticism – hence, the perception and acceptance of symbols and/or environmental stimuli may be 'socially filtered' through a genetic predisposition to respond to these symbols or stimuli. That is, disentangling environmental from genetic influences might not be even possible at all.

It is common belief within literature that most of the DNA structure is made up of 'junk' material – approx. 97% of it (Bryson, 2004) or 95% according to Davies (2001). This at first sight could mean less difficulty to find the genes that determine behaviour. However, the problem is that it would still take years just to isolate the genes responsible for behaviour themselves. Hence, the remaining 3-5% of 'useful' DNA still accounts for a combination of 3 billion chemical bases that constitutes humans. In addition, one needs to consider that a human being carries 46 chromosomes, each of them containing a complete DNA structure. The scientific consensus is that human personality is partially (50%) influenced by genetic inheritance and environmental influence (50%) (Mader,1995). Yet this information only adds to the complexity as here the concept of personality implies that behaviour follows a predictable pattern (see chapter 3 for counter argument). Moreover, the number of possibilities that arise when one considers the 50% probability of genetic inheritance that influence behaviour, put it simple, is flabbergasting – one first would have to identify which part of DNA in which chromosome carries the information about behaviour, then decode it, then understand how the process takes place, then work out the human behavioural expression possibilities, which would only be possible through the understanding of other 'pack of genes' that would be related to it and influence the final behavioural outcome (e.g. the genes that determine taste). This is only for one person. Multiply the procedure by 6 billion people (or the number of people from a segment; some millions, for instance) and the enterprise that involves very complex statistical analysis becomes literally overwhelming. Not to forget the other 50% environmental influence on people's behaviour. The arguments above are bolstered by Carson & Rothstein (1999) who suggest that complex traits (e.g. behavioural traits) are determined by interactions between many genes and environmental factors; and DiLalla (2004 pp85) who highlights that "Despite popular press reports that sporadically trumpet the discovery of specific genes "for" particular personality traits, it bears repeating that genetic influences on personality and psychopathology are likely to be multifactorial rather than Mendelian (Eaves, Eysenck, & Martin, 1989; Gottesman, 1991, 2002; Loehlin, 1992) and may be nonadditive (Finkel & McGue, 1997)".

Despite the arduous procedure that the identification of genes responsible for behavioural traits carries with itself, there have been findings from researches suggesting specific chromosomes as the locus where behavioural disorders may be mediated or predetermined (Carson & Rothstein, 1999). However, these findings are much more related to pathologies than to 'normal' behavioural traits and also there seem to be contradictions about which chromosome bears the specific mutant gene that determines a disease. Furthermore, such uncertain findings would be of little help for the understanding of consumer behaviour – unless one could argue that understanding of compulsive behaviour could be helpful for companies to increase their sales turnover due to the exploitation of people's psychopathologic condition. There is no need to highlight here the dubious ethicality or even the unacceptability of such an approach. Furthermore, as Carson & Rothstein (1999 pp56) would put it: "The continued challenge will be to refine and dissect the phenotypes [external biological traits] of behavioural traits and psychiatric disorders to facilitate the identification of putative genes and to uncover their complicated interactions with the environment". Again, whether this suggested 'refinement' and 'dissection' of behavioural traits and its associations with these 'complicated interactions with the environment' can be achieved (with all the development in technology and human genetics) is yet to be found out.

In June 2000 it has been announced by the scientists Francis Collins and J.C. Venter that the human genome (the complete sequence of a 3-billion chemical basis of human DNA – 'the complete instruction manual of humans') had been achieved - some 15 years after the sequencing work started. Genetics has heavily been applied to understand about diseases such as Huntington's and cancer, which genes carry the information that may trigger their development, and about heredity of phenotypic (e.g. morphologic traits) traits amongst family members and/or their implications to future genetic disorders development (Bryson, 2004; Davies, 2001; Marteau & Richards, 1996; Mader, 1995). In the same fashion, some people are believed to be predisposed to addictions such as alcoholism, which according to Guerrini et al (2005), 60% of it is originated through heritability. The links to the genes responsible for the occurrence of alcoholism are found in chromosomes 1p22.1-11.2 region, in contrast to the previously thought chromosomes 11, 4, 7 and in accordance with chromosome 1 suggested in other US studies. From such studies one can begin to grasp how complex the identification of genes and their relations to a specific aspect of a human behaviour disorder (alcoholism in this case) are, let alone the understanding of how the processes take place and provoke pathologic conditions. The reaching of the complete human genome may indeed be of great help for the development of new medicines and the cure for inherited pathologies in the long-term future and, unfortunately, for other controversial scientific procedures.

One cannot discard the possibility that it will also offer the premise of a way for other social disciplines such as marketing to enquire about human behaviour. Although, if so, there still is an enormous amount of expensive research to be done in order for marketers to start to understand how genes may determine human behaviour and, more importantly, how to use such knowledge to develop marketing strategies. It can become a far too expensive endeavour that even giant corporations may not afford. And if one considers that some companies may afford it, such corporations would have to face the ethical challenges (Marteau & Richards, 1996) that may emerge from society (e.g. Government policies, independent bodies and the population as a whole), and that taking on such an approach may damage their brand image amongst costumers. In addition, research in this area is just in its childhood and the more research is done the more the findings reveal deeper levels of complexity related to human behaviour.

One would engage in this risky enterprise at their own peril, as the results in the end may be very much disappointing and useless for marketers. Furthermore, even if the complete understanding about how genes influence behaviour was reached, this would only mean 'half way through' for the overall understanding of behaviour, since 50% of its causes seems to arise from the social environment.

As Davies (2001) would put it, the human genome 'has been cracked' and although the challenge now is to understand what this sequence means, according to him scientists have the potential of rewriting the human DNA sequence; the 'language of God'. A quite naïve statement, one could say, since there is a book of 3 billion letters not only to be read, but also to be fully understood and yet scientists have been trying to find solutions through the reading of some paragraphs of the book and, very probably, they might be missing the plot in the end. It will be years before humans grasp some understanding of it and by then, some of the 'junk' DNA may turn out not be junk at all - actually, it has already turned out so contemporary. This along with all that has been said so far gives only limited hope to the search for genetic explanations of human behaviour. It has become quite clear that one would need to address the possible differences between Christians and non-Christians in this respect, given that it could become plausible to speculate as to whether a predisposition to altruism or loving (which could explain the willingness to help other people) is determined by specific genes. Then again, whatever the outcome may be, it is fairly certain that it will not turn up exclusively in Christians. Neither will it guarantee that a person would engage in ethical purchasing behaviour because of that.

Mathematicians are our remaining hope. Can we calculate the effects of belief on consumer decision making? It seems unlikely, but let us see things from a mathematical perspective in the next chapter.

Chapter 6

Looking at Marketing from a Mathematical Perspective

In chapters 3, 4 and 5, psychological, ethical and biological perspectives have shed little useful light on the paradox and dilemma that were surfaced in chapter 1. Can the clear cold light of mathematical perspective illuminate things more usefully?

Bird (1999 pp.32) highlights that "the probability of something happening is the likelihood or chance of it happening". Francis (1996) affirms that the measure of the likelihood of a random event to occur on a scale between 0 and 1 is called probability. Mustoe & Barry (1998) says that probability theory is related to real situations in life that takes place as an action or an experiment of which the outcome is uncertain. When an experiment happens, this is defined as a random experiment which in turn is comprised of a set of possible outcomes. This set (S) of possible outcomes is named sample space and the sample space in turn is formed by a series of outcomes called, each of them, a sample point. Finally, an event is a cluster of sample points within a sample space (Mustoe & Barry, 1998) – in other words, an event is a combination of factors that leads to an uncertain outcome. Croft & Davison (1999) highlight that when an event is impossible the probability of it taking place is close to 0; when it is possible, the probability is close to 1 - the closer to 1. The higher the probability of an event to happen with 1 representing the absolute certainty of a given event to happen. According to these authors the majority of events are neither impossible nor certain. It is from this logical inference that the formula $0 \leq P(E) \leq 1$ derives, where $P(E)$ denotes the probability of an event to happen. It is common sense within the literature that the definition of events can be classified as *not mutually exclusive* and *mutually exclusive* and *dependent* and *independent events* (Bird, 1999; Croft & Davison, 1999; Mustoe & Barry, 1998; Francis, 1996; Fetner, 1996; Owe & Jones, 1994). With the *mutually exclusive* concept, the probability of two events to happen at the same, it can be said, is precisely 0. Regarding the *not mutually exclusive* concept, the probability of two events to take place at the same time stays within the 0-1 scale. The *dependent* event concept says that the probability of an event happening has an effect on the probability of another event happening, the *independent* concept says that the probability of two events do not affect one another. In the case of consumer behaviour studies, it is therefore possible to say that the 'purchase events' that happen amongst a group of different people can be classified as both mutually and not mutually exclusive, since the purchase of a specific product may or may not happen at the same time by the same person or by different ones. It can also be said that quotidian 'purchase events' amongst different people are independent events, given that the probability of a purchase of, say, a fair-trade product by a Christian may not dependent on a previous Christian's purchase nor may it be dependent on the fact that the person is a Christian. However, it could not be said that they are mutually exclusive events as the buying of a fair-trade good by a Christian does not discard the probability of a non-Christian to buy it. Furthermore, if one considers the example of an individual that decides to cook for dinner 'Spaghetti Bolognese', the buying (events) of mincemeat and pasta are dependent (events) on one another or they are not mutually exclusive, given that without mincemeat and pasta, spaghetti Bolognese cannot be made.

These possible different ways of seeing a 'purchase event' indicates that marketing research (or any social research) on consumer behaviour that only relies upon statistical analysis are passive of unreliability, as depending on the circumstances where the event occur and the variables that influence (it is impossible for a researcher to control all social variables that can influence a 'purchase event') such an event as well as on the standpoint a research adopts - their results may lead to misinterpretations of reality, given that the same research findings may offer different probabilistic results. One reason for it would be if the discernment between mutually exclusive and not mutually exclusive and dependent and independent events is done wrongly. As a consequence, one could easily make use of the addition law to find out the probability of *not mutually exclusive* events or the multiplication law to find out the probability of dependent events. In both cases the probability results would be incorrect. Finally, even if the correct application of the concepts is made, one still would come up with different measures of probability depending upon the perspective adopted.

Mustoe & Barry (1998) affirm that the two ways of ascertain the probability of an event are the theoretical and experimental approaches and this affirmation is bolstered by Francis (1996). Owe & Jones (1994) call the theoretical and experimental approaches as *a priori* and *empirical* approaches respectively. In addition, these authors offer a third concept which is termed as the *subjective* approach to probability. Owe & Jones affirm that the *a priori* can be used only if one knows, before an experiment takes place, all possible outcomes of an event and weight the probability of the outcomes proportionally to their likelihood. The empirical approach is only possible if a (random) sample is drawn to bolster its significance, however, in real life circumstances (e.g. to find the probability of Christians to buy a fair trade product in comparison to a non-Christian) the empirical approach can only be reliable if the same, say 'purchase event', be repeated various times under identical conditions. The subjective approach is inextricably related to a personal estimation of the probability of an event to happen.

> "These three distinct approaches to probability raise an interesting philosophical problem. We know that *P(E)* can never exceed one, but does *P(E)* = 1 imply absolute certainty? It all depends on the approach used. If we use an *a priori* approach then *P(E)* = 1 means that *E must always occur.* However, using an empirical approach *P(E)* = 1 means that *E has always occurred* – which does not imply that it must occur in the future. Likewise, using a subjective approach *P(E)* = 1

> means that we *think that E will occur* – which again does not imply that it must occur" (Owe & Jones, 1994 pp 221).

From the above statement some conclusions can be drawn. Firstly, it is clear that an *a priori* approach to find out the probability of Christians and non-Christians to buy fair-trade products cannot be applied, since previous knowledge of possible outcomes is not possible to be achieved for all possible circumstances and/or sample space, unless one takes the very simplistic way of seeing a purchase similar to a throwing of a coin – it is either head (happens) or tail (not). In the same fashion, an empirical approach would only help to determine the probability of the same event to occur (e.g. the buying of a fair trade product by Christians and non-Christians) based on the fact that such an event has always happened in the past – hence even if the possible outcomes were known previously by marketers or they found out, based on last month's events, that the probability of Christians buying a fair trade product were higher than non-Christians that would not guarantee 100% certainty of the same probability to occur again or even be higher than the probability of non-Christians buying the same product in the future. This is because human behaviour is not immune from environmental influences, which in turn can change and exert a change in behaviour accordingly (e.g. hypothetically, what would happen if people found out that Fair Trade was created by Nike or GAP?). Moreover, marketers would never be able to guarantee that the conditions, where the sample of the study of this nature came from, were identical. At the best the subjective approach is the only way (though an ill way) to have a reasonable estimate of a commercial event to occur more than once based on market experience. Yet, consumers' behaviour is erratic and fickle and can be conditioned by elements such as personal mood, financial situation, weather conditions, desire for innovation, peer pressure, family influences, social status, educational background, beliefs, perception, transport system, product availability, quality, price and knowledge of its existence, health status (people may be on a diet or may be allergic to a product), taste, security issues…and the list goes on. One could estimate the probability of a purchase event to happen again based on previous data, but they would neither be able to guarantee that the event will occur again nor would they be able to explain whether (considering that a Christian bought repeatedly a fair-trade good in the past) a repeated purchase took place because the buyer was a Christian or they simply, say, liked the taste of it; or the packaging of it; or the cause that it bolsters; or the quality of it; or the availability of it; or the fact that there was only that product in the shop, etc. Thus, it is plausible to say that applying the statistical law of 'mass behaviour' to measure the probability of a 'purchase event' (e.g. the buying of fair trade goods) involving people from a certain social group (e.g. Christians) is at best a limited way of helping to see the 'whole picture'.

To better illustrate the previous arguments, let us take the example of Britain. Consider that the measure of probability can be achieved through previously known data. According to Mintel's (2005) report, 30 million British would consider themselves Christians (whether they are practising Christians is not here in question, nor is it relevant for the purpose of the following arguments, since is the logic of the arguments that are to be highlighted and not the accuracy of probabilistic measures). Since Britain has approx. 59.3 million inhabitants, it is possible to reach the conclusion that approx. 1 in 2 persons of the population are Christians or that the probability of a random person to be a Christian is 0.5. From this information one could straightforwardly conclude that in a random supermarket a random person who buys a fair-trade product has 50% chance of being a Christian. Therefore, one could assume that the probability of a non-

Christian buying that fair-trade product is 0.5 also or there is a 50% chance that it occurs. And the same logic would be applicable to all others who bought a fair trade good. Inasmuch as what has been said, the events could easily be seen as *mutually exclusive*, since a person could not be Christian and non-Christian at the same time – it would be either one or the other. However, the purchase of a fair-trade product would have to be associated to the person's status and if there is more than one person buying the same product the events become *not mutually exclusive* even if there are Christians and non-Christians involved at the same time in the purchases. Yet, the events could be seen as independent given that the probability of a purchase of a fair-trade product by a Christian is not dependent on the probability of a purchase of a fair trade good by a non-Christian. Therefore, here not only a statistical impossibility becomes possible, but also it can offer two different probability measures based on the same event.

Considering what has been said before, even if the results of a study indicated that Christians would be more likely to buy fair-trade goods, this would not guarantee that they bought such goods because they are Christians but, perhaps, because fair-trade products are distributed through Christian organisations/institutions and it just happens that non-Christians have less access to these products. So, organisations could just as well be indirectly biasing their very same marketing research findings. In addition, from two different researched places in Britain where, say, the concentration of Christians is higher the non-Christians, the probability measures from both researches would show different results for the very same event, the purchase of a fair-trade product by a Christian or non-Christian. Therefore, the results could never be generalised as being representative of the British reality and, if so, it could potentially bias marketing strategy choices and refrain an organisation from increasing its market share. Researches based on an *empirical* approach would show results that only indicate that at a specific point in time, in a specific place and with a specific sub-sample of the British population, a specific probabilistic measure could be estimated. Since applying the law of 'mass behaviour' to measure the probability of such social events would also be misleading, probabilistic inferences would be of little help for marketers to fairly predict whether Christians would be more likely to buy fair trade products than non-Christians. This logic can be applied outside the British sample example and the conclusions about the measure of probability of purchase events will be the same.

In summary, it is reasonable to say that measures of probability involving purchase events offer limited help to marketers trying to predict whether (in this case) Christians would be more likely to buy fair-trade products than non-Christians. There seems little reason why marketers should concentrate their efforts on marketing fair-trade goods to only Christians as, if an *a priori* approach to probability is taken, the conclusion will be that there is a fifty-fifty probability for Christians and non-Christians to buy fair-trade goods. If an *empirical* approach is taken, the conclusion will be that specific results cannot be generalised given that real life social events are ever changing and so the experiment cannot be repeated under identical conditions. If a *subjective* approach to probability is taken, then marketers might as well trust in their 'gut feelings' and experiential knowledge when devising their marketing strategies. If so, one could question whether marketing literature about consumer behaviour is of great help for marketers at all.

The results from looking at marketing from four perspectives have been recorded in the previous four chapters. But what do they really mean? What ideas can we infer? What do these ideas imply for marketers?

Chapter 7

Discussion

In the previous four chapters, four different subjects were explored, searching for insights into whether there are any theoretical standpoints which bolster the hypothesis in the case study that Christians would be more likely to buy fair trade products than non-Christians. Applying critical thinking to theories from within psychology, ethics, biology and mathematics, as they might bear on our case study, we have recorded some interesting observations and some tentative insights. But what separately, or even better, collectively, do they all mean? Is there anything we can now say we really know? Is it really true? Is there some general truth or principles that we could infer? It is to these questions that this discussion chapter now turns.

"Marketing managers need to understand who their customers are in order to target their marketing activity as precisely as possible. Once they know who customers are, they also need to know as much as possible about how those customers behave. They would like to know what influences customers' decision and what processes they follow to select a product or service. They would particularly like to know how customers choose between one product and another, so that they could use that information to increase the chances of their own products being selected" (Stokes, 2002 pp104). One could say that this statement summarises what the studies about consumer behaviour aim at. It is nonetheless a very complex argument, since it highlights the need for marketers to know their customers to an extent of understanding how they would behave when it comes to the decision of purchasing a product - such assumption in turn also reveals some critical points, as it implies not only that human behaviour follows a constant or straightforward pattern and its prediction may be achievable through the understanding of customers (to the extent of knowing how they tend to behave in any purchase event), but also it implies that a cluster of customers may be targeted because they share similar traits (about which specifications are notably unspecific, at least as presented in books on marketing segmentation). These assumptions are common within marketing literature (Pickton & Broderick, 2005; Chernatony & McDonald, 2005; Belch & Belch, 2004; Jobber, 2004; Czinkota & Ronkainen, 2004; Kotler, 2003; Stokes, 2002). Nevertheless, from the psychological, ethical, biological and mathematical perspectives, the evidence points in a rather different direction when it comes to the possibility of understanding customers to an extent that one could guarantee or at least assume with a given certainty that a person will behave in a specific way just because they have some specific socio-psychological traits. It seems that, within the marketing literature here reviewed consumer behaviour is treated as a constant one-off or 'frozen' event, almost as if the same customer will tend to behave in the same manner every time, they buy goods. Undoubtedly one can find out what may influence a given customer's decision. However, to assume that knowing the processes which customers go through when choosing products to buy will indicate that such customers will tend to buy a specific product is a woefully unsupported assertion. Even if marketers know what influences customers to buy a specific product, it lends little help to improve marketing strategies, unless causality between customers' willingness to buy and their real reasons for it (say for example, a pack of coffee and personal taste) are established – hence, in the case of this study, even the assumption that a Christian would be influenced by their beliefs which are related to being compassionate, loving and acting ethically, does not indicate that they will act in such ways.

It could be argued that one way to find out about the likelihood of Christians to buy a fair-trade product (for example) against non-Christians would be through empirical research which gathered enough data for statistically valid analysis. However, as shown in chapter 6, probability measures cannot only be deceiving, but also, at the most, they are nothing more than a reading at a specific time in a specific place and are unlike natural events which tend to conserve the same behavioural patterns (e.g. cells tend to behave in the same way repeatedly, unless they are ill). Marketing researchers should not claim that applying the 'mass behaviour' probabilistic approach to human beings will be a sound way of predicting the future behaviour of consumers.

A concept widely used in marketing is the 'black box', which assumes that everyone makes buying decisions within this so-called box, which in turn filters and absorbs internal and external influences. It is said that most of this process takes place in our conscious and sub-conscious (Stokes, 2002). "All we can do is observe what is happening around the individual or an organisation at the time of a buying decision and look at what inputs and influences the 'black box' might be receiving" (Stokes, 2002 pp105) – what real benefit can marketers have through the observation of an event that happens conditioned by specific elements in a specific time and sample space if the next event may be a completely different one altogether? Another concept frequently relied upon is the decision-making unit (DMU). DMUs are said to arise and be related to a group of people who play different roles during the decision-making process (Jobber, 2004; Kotler, 2003). The 'black box' theory is an interesting model that only highlights the complexity of human thought and the number of 'uncontrollable' variables that may influence it. Belch & Belch (2004) pinpoint other aspects related to decision-making processes such as motivation, perception, attitude, integration and learning process. They also highlight the cognitive paradigm which emphasises the stages one goes through when deciding to buy a product: problem recognition, information search, alternative evaluation, purchase decision and post-purchase evaluation. Pickton & Broderick (2005), suggest that independently of the differences between the cognitive and the behaviourist paradigms, customers go through pre-purchase, purchase, post-purchase evaluation and product disposal stages. Also, Czinkota & Ronkainen (2004), emphasise the need for cultural aspects to be considered by marketers, if they are to be successful in the international market. Hofstede's model (1984) which shows cultural differences amongst various countries based on four different variables: uncertainty avoidance (e.g. need for formal rules and regulations), power distance (e.g. level of equality in a society), masculinity (e.g. attitudes towards achievement, roles of men and women) and individualism (e.g. "I" consciousness versus "We" consciousness) - examples from Czinkota & Ronkainen. This model is worthy of deeper considerations. Firstly, the model suggests that results found in a specific sample and time frame from within specific parts of some specific countries can be generalised for the whole of each country. Secondly, all facets of the model are assumed to be still relevant, even though approx. 20 years have passed since the research took place on which it was based. The information provided about Brazilians (the author is a Brazilian) provides a counter argument. Take uncertainty avoidance in Brazil. Dealing with uncertainty is part of Brazilian culture and mentality. Given the ever-going economic instability of the country, corruption mentality of our politicians and of a great part of the population and the lack of consistent law enforcement throughout centuries, uncertainty is endemic. Taking risks without guarantees was and is part of Brazilians' quotidian (Caldeira, 2004; Dreyfus, 1997; Semler, 1994). Yet Brazilians score very high on uncertainty avoidance on Hofstede's model, above countries such as Germany, Netherlands and Great Britain. The author's personal living experience in Germany and England runs counter to the information provided on Hofstede's model. Brazil is composed of 27 states. Its structure is more like the federal structure in the USA. Its size and cultural variations is more like Europe. Its representation by Hofstede's model is simplistic. This in turn leads to other problems such as the determination of the level of individualism in a nation. Brazil, according to the model, scores below many European countries for individualism, and yet 'We consciousness', in many parts of the country is not high – try to queuing in a public organisation, at a bus stop, or get stuck in a traffic jam in many parts or look the state of public spaces. In Brazil one will quickly realise that "We" can have the meaning of "Me first". The idea of the collective is not a well-understood concept in the culture. Brazilian reality reflects the colonisation process that spread a mentality of selfishness and individualism through practices such as the establishment of *capitanias hereditarias*' (the right to inherit land) and land donations from the empire to entrepreneurs (Caldeira, 2004). Given the constant changes in the global environment (e.g. Globalisation and Internet) a model from nearly 20 years ago may not be based on reliable assumptions about present behaviour.

The marketing literature reviewed is very often based on theoretical socio-psychological descriptions and explanations of human traits and behaviour. Where attempts are made to bridge the gap between theory and practice, correlations are often assumed to be causes. Putting aside for the moment the reservations (and the grateful recognition) which has been ascribed to much of the academic work reviewed in chapters 3-6, attempts by market practitioners to translate the academic findings in valid and useful action were frequently found to be suspect. The capacity for drawing valid, relevant and significant inferences and practical implications for things to do (and avoid doing) seemed scarce. The literature neither adequately distinguishes nor directly addresses issues such as individual uniqueness. It is replete with cultural generalisations (e.g. Hofstede's model) and models for mass behaviour.

Take, for example, the marketers' concept of segmentation. The idea of segmentation is based on the assumption that customers are different from one another. This is internally inconsistent with the idea that one can then group these individuals into segments whose buying behaviours will be the same. The use of

Psychographics (related to costumers' personality, lifestyle or 'tribes', for example) to define marketing segments assumes that people can be allocated to groups whose buying decisions will be the same or at least similar. Yet, as shown in chapter 3, personality is not a readily generalisable label for individuals. There are not two individuals that are identical; be it from a psychological (chapter 3) or biological perspective (chapter 5). Not even research on identical twins has offered findings which point to 100% certainty in twins' traits similarities. The lack of understanding of the motivation for customers' buying decisions means that correlations are again assumed to be causal, so that, in reality, practitioners have no grounds for assuming either that lifestyle is a consequence of personality traits or that personality traits are influenced by lifestyle. Is the belonging to a specific social group a characteristic or consequence, of personality traits? Or are they conditioned, or not, by the result difficulties in social ascension? One may be a poor person without formal education and yet behave like people in socio-economically affluent groups. They may buy expensive products, even by sacrificing other priorities.

The use of demographic criterion has been given a statistical veneer of science (chapter 6). Yet, one does not have to be a scientist to predict that adults will not pay for a pair of trousers made for kids, nor that men will normally not buy bras for themselves. It is self-evident that people who like or practise a sport are more likely to buy a product related to that sport. One does not need the tools of rocket science to predict that customers will prefer products that have reasonably low price, high reliability and safety that is easily available and enhances one's social status. There is evidence that customers prefer products that offer value for money and that they primarily search for good quality, reliability and convenience when considering buying a product (Carrigan et al, 2004; Carrigan & Attallan, 2001; Shaw & Clarke, 1999; Yam-Tang & Chan, 1998) – Unsurprisingly, our case study concluded that even if products were held to be ethical, they would not stand a chance in the market if they did not satisfy these elementary (at least some of them) conditions. But if they met these conditions, they would not need to be ethically correct to succeed.

The Case Study concerned the likelihood of Christians buying fair-trade products, based on the assumption that because of their beliefs Christians would be more willing to buy goods which guaranteed fair wages for producers from developing countries. However, not one of the perspectives reviewed lends support to this hypothesis. The findings of critical thinking analysis in chapters 3-6 give us no grounds, from the perspective psychology, ethics, biology or mathematics, that Christians would be any more likely to buy fair-trade products than any other consumers. Such a phenomenon is much more likely to arise because of the way fair-trade products are distributed: i.e. mainly through Christian institutions. One needs not to be Christian to be affected by appeals to compassion, love and social injustice. The relatively constant increase in sales of fair-trade products is more likely to be the result of improving quality and availability (Cowe & Williams, 2000). The motivation for these purchases may still not lie in beliefs at all. There is no evidence that Christians make up the majority of fair-trade buyers. The emphasis that has been placed by selling organisations on the ethicality of fair-trade goods as a marketing alibi is precarious, perishable and expensive to maintain and sustain. It also seems to be an unnecessary waste of resources. As a bi-product it places the livelihoods of those meant to benefit from the fair trade at higher risk. If the economic and charitable scaffolding, that shores up the price or preference for their fairly traded product, collapses (or eve wanes) then is the producers and pickers who will suffer. Our Case Study revealed no support for the belief that Christians (or non-Christians) based their purchase decision making on ethical choice, ethical product or ethical behaviour. In addition, a latent question, about how ethical fair-trade products really are, lurks in the wings. Such trade is vulnerable to even one well publicised scandal about corruption in the systems by which fair trade labels are awarded.

That the outcome of the reviews turned out to be so negative and pessimistic about the usefulness of marketing to those who might benefit from fair trade, is very disappointing. In the recommendations chapter we hope to compensate for this disappointment by suggesting a new model and a more hopeful way forward. The model could be called SSTEP (Self Segmentation Through Extreme Paradox) and the emphasis could be on the (P) product which a company would intend to commercialise and where the other 'Ps' of Marketing were determined by the product (P) itself. In a nutshell, through a proposed SSTEP model, once the idea of a product (P) might be conceived, segments would self-develop in the market through the combination of elements such price, quality, information and product availability – not ethical considerations leading to religion or church-based distributions. Based on chapters 3-6, people appear to have unique psychological and genetic traits which cannot presently be understood to the extent necessary to predict human behaviour. People's 'uniqueness' are not easily treated collectively. There are powerful vested interests in getting us to believe that customer's decision making can be manipulated. Even the belief that customer's decision making can be manipulated through unethical means such as subliminal advertising techniques is questionable (Belch & Belch, 2004) and may be misplaced. In the end, it is the customer who chooses when and by whom to be influenced. Furthermore, as the reviews of the various perspectives considered in chapters 3-6 show, people who present specific and similar psychological traits, beliefs (e.g. religious) and attitudes (e.g. ethical) will neither necessarily behave in the same way, nor will they behave according to their beliefs and attitudes. On the other hand, there is evidence to believe that a product that combines the right elements of price, quality, availability and information will attract customers from traditionally defined demographic or socio-economic segments. Who are TESCO's customers, for instance? Is the Hawaii a destination only for young people? Chapters 3-6 do not support that the commercialisation of a product should depend on discriminative segmentation in order for it to be successful in the market. There appear to be buyers from all sorts of 'segments' that will buy a product as long as it offers the right combination between price, quality, information and availability. Such critical reasoning implies that marketers should avoid trying to understand a market composed of segments and should concentrate on improving that which they can control.

Chapter 8

Main Conclusions

The critical analysis, based on the four different perspectives reported in chapters 3-6 and discussed in the previous chapter 7 made use of the Case Study about Christians' likelihood to buy fair-trade products. The case assumed that because of their beliefs Christians would be more likely to buy such goods, since fair-trade goods are represented ethically correct and said to guarantee fair wages for producers from developing countries. However, not one of the perspectives reviewed bolstered this ideia.

- From a philosophical and theoretical standpoint taken in four major bodies of knowledge (psychology, ethics, biology and mathematics), critical analysis does not support the idea that Christians would be more likely to buy fair-trade products.

- What is more likely to explain the phenomenon of increasing purchases of fair-trade goods by Christians (if such a phenomenon there be) is the way fair-trade products are distributed, i.e. mainly through Christian institutions.
- The increase in sales of fair-trade products is more likely to be due the increase in quality and availability of the products (Cowe & Williams, 2000).
- The emphasis that has been placed by organisations on the ethicality of fair-trade goods as a marketing alibi is precarious, perishable and probably unsustainable.
- People have unique psychological and genetic "traits" which cannot presently be understood to the extent necessary to predict or shape human behaviour.
- It is unhelpful to try and respond to 'uniqueness' by the collectivisation idea implicit in many approaches to market segmentation.
- People who present similar psychological traits, beliefs (e.g. religious) and attitudes (e.g. ethical) will not necessarily behave in the

same way (nor will they behave in accordance with their beliefs and attitudes!).

- Products that combine the right elements of price, quality, availability and information are as likely to attract customers from all demographic and socio-economic segments of society as products that are promoted as ethical or fair trade.

- The marketing of products generally (including ethical and fair-trade products) could be rendered more effective by changing present approaches to market segmentation to ones in which marketers concentrate on variables over which they can exercise some control.

Such change would be helped by a new model of market segmentation, for instance.

Chapter 9

Recommendations

The case study approach was based on the epistemological stance of interpretivism with a methodology based on critical analysis within a philosophical paradigm. Engaging in a philosophical process that involved four major bodies of knowledge (psychology, biology, ethics and mathematics) the author has tried to explore aspects relevant to consumer behaviour, using the case study of Christians and Fair Trade. This work cannot be claimed to be exhaustive. Other perspectives exist and were not chosen. The reasons for choosing psychology, ethics, biology and mathematics reflected personal interests of the author. The lack of other perspectives reflected expediency and pragmatic pressures of time and return-for-effort. Had perspectives from physics, economics and politics been included, for example, the outcome of the critical analysis might have been different. That might be for future critical theorists and researchers to determine. The work has other weaknesses. For instance, many

Cartesians would say that its results ought not to be applied generally. It does not claim to offer representative sampling nor does it offer statistically significant findings. Yet Socratic logic long predates modernist science, as a means of identifying generalisable truths or hypothesis, by thinking critically about a single example. Another criticism would be that the interpretation is biased by the author's worldview. This criticism is accepted. That is why the proper product of critical analysis is often further questions to be explored. Here a new model of market segmentation is offered. This new model should itself be tested for relevance and utility.

Furthermore, the intention here was not to reject any scientists' contribution made to present understanding but to embrace their findings and to try to explore the question from the scientists' different perspectives. Marketing sits within the management paradigm in which an espoused 'science' of management has often seen a veneer of science being placed over what is an essentially socially mediated process. The implicit hope was that any fallacies inherent in this might be exposed. This may have led to bias.

It is suggested that research on the same subject involving both qualitative and quantitative methods be carried out in order for the present research findings to be verified with more accuracy.

This research process has produced a new model - a different way of addressing the concept of marketing segmentation. It is through the empirical application of such model that subsequent testing and validation can be achieved. The author hopes for and welcomes scientific initiatives which can contribute to the development and improvement of the proposed model that has emerged from this research. The model is presented in figure 1 (below).

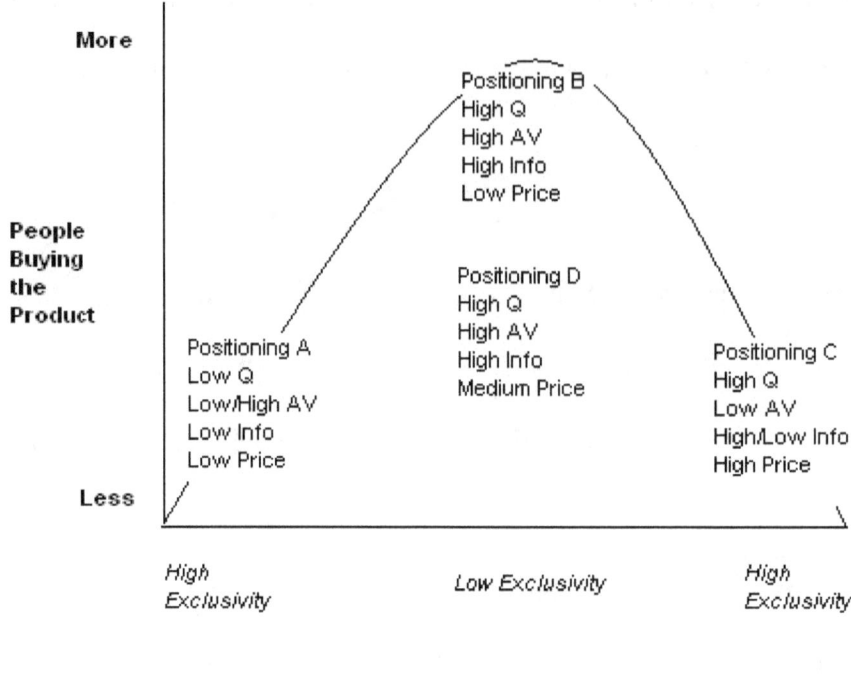

Figure 1 – The proposed SSTEP Model of Market Segmentation (Silva, 2005).

The principle on which the SSTEP model is proposed is related to the idea that combinations of products' price and quality, product availability and product information self-segment a market. The product can become a 'mass' product (little tailored or exclusive), or it can become an 'exclusive product', for very few people (very much tailored or exclusive). One paradox is that when a product that is launched in the market with very low product information, low quality, low product availability and high or low price, it becomes a 100% tailored product (even if the intention by marketers would be to market the product as non-tailored or for the 'mass'). The model shows that depending on how marketers 'play' with price, quality, product and information availability, marketers will attract the people who are willing to comply with a given product specification. Products that are extremely expensive, have high quality, low or high product information, low or high product availability, are 100% tailored. However, if the price element is changed, the product may shift to close 0% tailored. One way or the other, there is the possibility that the product may be sold. The difference is that the type of customers will be different. The profits in the end may be the same, provided the lower price is sufficiently greater than the variable cost, since the increased number of people buying lower price/less tailored products may make up for the fewer people who would have spent more to buy a more tailored/exclusive product.

The author recommends that the SSTEP model be developed into a useful tool for marketers or simply for entrepreneurs of SMEs who do not have enough resources to engage in comprehensive marketing approaches. Like all new tools it should be used with caution and, for the moment, in parallel with existing tools until it can be modified or used with confidence to replace models of segmentation that are based on false assumptions and fallacious reasoning.

Bibliography

Alreck, P.L. & Settle, R.B. (1999), **Strategies for building consumer brand preference**, *Journal of Product & Brand Management*, Vol.8 No.2 pp130-144

Ball, D., Coelho, P.S. & Machas, A. (2003), **The role of communication and trust explaining customer loyalty**, *European Journal of Marketing*, Vol.38 No 9/10 pp.1272-1293

Beauchamp, T.L. & Bowie, N.E. (2004), **Ethical Theory and Business**, (7th Ed), Pearson Education International, New Jersey

Belch, E.G & Belch, M.A. (2004), **Advertising and Promotion**, (6th Ed.), McGraw Hill, Boston

Benn, P. (1998), **Ethics**, UCL press, London

Berg, B.L.(2001), **Qualitative Research Methods for the Social Sciences**, (4th Ed.), Allyn and Bacon, London

Bhaskaran, S. & Hardley, F. (2002), **Buyer beliefs, attitudes and behaviour: foods with therapeutic claims**, *Journal of Consumer Marketing*, Vol.19 No 7 pp. 591-606

Bird, J.(1999), **Higher Engineering Mathematics**, (3rd Ed), Newnes, Oxford

Blackstock, J.C. (1998), **Biochemistry**, Butterworth-Heinemann, Oxford

Boxer, P. & Tisak, M.S. (2003), **Adolescents' attributions about aggression: an initial investigation**, *Journal of Adolescents (science direct)*, No 26 pp. 559-573

Brink-Budgen, R.van den (2003), **Critical Thinking for Students**, (3rd E.), Howtobooks, Oxford

Bryson, B. (2004), **A Short History of Nearly Everything**, Black Swan, London

Blythe, J. (1997), **The Essence of Consumer Behaviour**, Prentice-Hall, Harlow

Brownie, A.C. & Kernohan, J.C.(1999), **Biochemistry**, Churchill Livingstone, Edinburgh

Cahn, S.T. & Markie, P.(1998), **Ethics: History, Theory, and Contemporary Issues**, Oxford University Press, Oxford

Caldeira, J. (2004), Maua' Empresario do Imperio, (24th Ed.), Companhia Das Letras, Sao Paulo

Carson, R.A. & Rothstein, M.A. (1999), **Behavioural Genetics: The Clash of Culture and Biology**, The Johns Hopkins University Press, London

Carrigan, M. & Attala, A. (2001), **The myth of the ethical consumer – do ethics matter in purchase behaviour**, *Journal of Consumer Marketing*, Vol.18 No 7 pp.560-577

Carrigan, M., Szmigin & Wright, J. (2004), **Shopping for a better world? An interpretive study of the potential for ethical consumption within the older market**, *Journal of Consumer Marketing*, Vol.21 No6 pp.401-417

Cassel, C. & Symon, G. (2004), **Essential Guide to Qualitative Methods in Organizational Research**, Sage Publications, London

Chapman, G. (1994), **Catechism of the Catholic Church**, Cassel, London

Chatel, F. (2003), **Creati in dono, dialogando su: la sfida del modello persona**,

Grafica Romana, Rome

Chernatony, L. de & McDonald, M. (2005), **Creating Powerful Brands**, (3rd Ed.), Elsevier, Oxford

Christopher, M., Payne, A. & Ballantyne, D. (2002), **Relationship Marketing**, Butter-Heinemann, Oxford

Cowe, R. & Williams, S. (2000), **Who are the ethical consumers?**, The Cooperative Bank, England

Cova, B. & Cova V. (2002), **Tribal marketing: The tribalisation of society and its impact on the conduct of marketing**, *European Journal of Marketing*, Vol.36, No.5/6 pp.595-620

Craig, C.S. & Douglas, S.P. (2001), **Conducting international research in the twenty-first century**, *International Marketing Review*, Vol.18 No.1 pp.80-90

Croft, A. & Davison, R.(1999), **Mathematics for Engineers: a modern interactive approach**, Addison Wesley, Harlow

Czinkota, M.R & Ronkainen, I.A. (2004), **International Marketing**, (7th Ed.), Thomson Learning, USA

Davies, K. (2001), **The Sequence: Inside the Race for the Human Genome**, Weidenfeld & Nicolson, London

Deci, E.L. (1976), **Intrinsic Motivation**, (2nd Ed), Plenum Press, New York

Delener, N. (1994), **Religious Contrasts in Consumer Decision Behaviour Patterns: Their Dimensions and Marketing Implications**, *European Journal of Marketing*, Vol.28 No5 pp.36-53

Denzin, N. & Lincoln, Y.(2000), **Handbook of Qualitative Research**, Sage Publications, London

DiLalla, L.F. (2004), **Behaviour Genetics Principles: Perspectives in Development, Personality, and Psychopathology**, American Psychological Association, Washington DC

Dreyfus, D.(1997), Vida do Viajante: A Saga de Luiz Gonzaga, (2nd Ed.), Editora 34, Sao Paulo

Duncan, T. (2002), **IMC – Using Advertising and Promotion to Build Brands**, McGraw-Hill, London

Evans, P. (1975), **Motivation**, Methuen, London

Fentem, R. (1996), **Statistics**, Collins Educational, London

Ferrand, A. & Pages, M. (1999), **Image management in sport organisations: the creation of value**, *European Journal of Marketing*, Vol. 33 No3/4, pp. 387-401

Fisher, A.(2003), **Critical Thinking**, (2nd Ed.), Cambridge University Press, Cambridge

Foxall, G.R., Goldsmith, R.E. & Brown, S. (1998), **Consumer Psychology for Marketing**, (2nd Ed), International Thomson Business, London

Francis, B. (1996), **Pure Mathematics**, Collins Educational, London

Gabbott, M. and Hogg, G. (1997), **contemporary Services Marketing Management**, The Dryden Press, London

Green, R.M. (1994), **The Ethical Manager**, Macmillan College, USA

Groenroos, C. (2000), **Service Management and Marketing**, (2nd Ed.), Wiley, Chichester

Guerrini, I., Cook, C.C.H., Kest, W., Devitgh, A., Mcquillin, A., Curtis, D., Gurling, H.M.D. (2005), **Genetic linkage analysis supports the presence of two susceptibility loci for alcoholism and heavy drinking on chromosome 1p22.1-11.2 and 1q21.3-24.2**, *BMC Genetics*, 6:11 doi:10.1186/1471-2156-611

Gummesson, E. (2001), **Total Relationship Marketing: Rethinking Marketing Management: From 4Ps to 30Rs**, Butterworth-Heinemann, Oxford

Hoffman, K.G. & Bateson, J.E.G (2002), **Essential of Services Marketing: Concepts, Strategies & Cases**, (2nd Ed.), Harcourt College Publications, Orlando

Horne, T. & Wootton, S.(2005), **Human Thinking**, UK

Hughes, J. (1990), **The Philosophy of Social Research**, (2nd Ed.), Longman Group Ltd, Essex

Jobber, D. (2004), **Principles and Practice of Marketing**, (4th Ed), McGraw-Hill, London

Kiesler, C. A., Collins, B. E. and Miller, N. (1969), **Attitude Change: a critical**

analysis of theoretical approaches, John Wiley & Sons, London

Killian, K. & Perez, F. (1998), **Ricardo Semler and Semco S.A.**, *The American Graduate School of International Management,* pp.1-9

Kotler, P. (2003), **Marketing Management**, (11th Ed.), Pearson Education, New Jersey

Lovelock, C. H. and Wright, L. (2002), **Principles of Service Marketing and Management**, (2nd Ed.), Prentice Hall, New Jersey

Low, J & Durkin, K. (2001), **Children's conceptualization of law enforcement on television and in real life**, *Legal and Criminological Psychology*, No 6 pp. 197-214

Mader, S.S. (1995), **Human Biology**, (4th Ed), WCB, Dubuque

Marteau, T. & Richards, M.(1996), **The Troubled Helix: social and psychological implications of the new human genetics**, Cambridge University Press, Cambridge

May, T. (2001), **Social Research - issues, methods and process**, (3rd Ed.), Open University Press, Buckingham - Philadelphia

Middleton, V.T.C. and Clarke, J. (2001), **Marketing in Travel and Tourism**, (3rd Ed.), Butterworth-Heinemann, Oxford

Mintel (2005), **Religious Tourism – International – March 2005**, *Mintel International Group Limited*, UK

Mowen, J.C. & Minor, M. (1998), **Consumer Behaviour**, (5th Ed), Prentice-Hall, New Jersey

Mustoe, L.R. & Barry, M.D.J.(1998), **Mathematics in Engineering and Science**, Wiley, Chichester

Norman, R. (1998), **The Moral Philosophers**, (2nd Ed), Oxford University Press, Oxford

O'Shaughnessy, J. & O'Shaughnessy, N.J.(2002), **Marketing, the consumer society and hedonism**, *European Journal of Marketing*, Vol.36 No5/6 pp.524-547

Owen, F. & Jones, R.(1994), **Statistics**, (4th Ed), Pitman, London

Padgett, D.K. (1998), **Qualitative Methods in Social Work: challenges and rewards**, SAGE, London

Parkinson, B. & Colman, A.M. (1995), **Emotion and Motivation**, Longman, London

Parrott, W.G. (2001), **Emotions in Social Psychology**, Psychology Press, Philadelphia

Persegani, C., Russo, P., Carucci, C., Nicolini, M., Papeschi, L.L., Trimarchi, M. (2001), **Television viewing and personality structure in children**, *Personality and Individual Differences (Elsevier)*, No 32 pp. 977-990

Piaget, J. (2001), **The Psychology of Intelligence**, Lodon, Routledge

Pickton, D. & Broderick, A. (2005), **Integrated Marketing Communications**, (2nd Ed.), Prentice Hall, London

Raviv, A., Raviv, A & Shimoni, H. (1999), **Children's self-report of exposure to violence and its relation to emotional distress**, *Journal of Applied Developmental Psychology (Elsevier)*, No 20 pp. 337-353

Reeve, J. (2005), **Understanding Motivation and Emotion** (4th Ed), Wiley, Iowa

Rosenkoetter, L.I., Rosenkoetter, S.E., Ozretich, R.A., Acock, A.C. (2004), **Mitigating the harmful effects of violent television**, *Applied Developmental Psychology (Elsevier)*, No 25 pp. 25-47

Rose, S., Lewontin, R.C. & Kamin, L.J. (1985), **Not In Our Genes: Biology, Ideology and Human Nature**, (2nd Ed), Penguin Books Ltd, Middlesex

Sarantakos, S. (1998), **Social Research**, (2nd Ed.), Macmillan Press Ltd, London

Saunders, M., Lewis, P. & Thornhill, A. (1997), **Research Methods for Business Students**, Pitman Publishing, Basingstoke

Seale, C. (2000), **The Quality of Qualitative Research**, SAGE, London

Semler, R. (1994), **Maverick! The success story behind the world's most unusual workplace**, Arrow, London

Shaffer, D.R. (2002), **Developmental Psychology: childhood & adolescence**, (6th Ed.), Wadsworth, United Kingdom

Shaw, D. & Clarke, I. (1999), **Belief formation in ethical consumer groups: an exploratory study**, *Marketing Intelligence & Planning*, Vol. 17 No2 pp.109-119

Shaw, W.H. (1999), **Contemporary Ethics**, Taking Account of Utilitarianism, Blackwell Publishers, Oxford

Shiffman, L.G. & Kanuk, L.L. (1999), **Consumer Behaviour**, (7th Ed.), Prentice Hall, London

Silva, M.A. (2004), **Devoted Football Fans: what's in their minds?**, *Dissertation for the MA in Sport Management*, University of Central Lancashire, Preston

Silverman, D. (2001), **Interpreting Qualitative Data: methods for analysing, talk, text and interaction**, (2nd Ed.), SAGE, London

Singer, P.(1994), **Ethics**, Oxford University Press, Oxford

Solomon, M.R. (2002), **Consumer Behaviour**, (5th Ed), Prentice-Hall International, New Jersey

Stanford, P. (2005), **The Catholic Church**, *BBC Religion & Ethics*, www.bbc.co.uk

Steenkamp J. E.M. (2001), **The role of national culture in international marketing research**, *International Marketing Review*, Vol.18 No.1 pp.30-44

Sterba, J.P.(1998), **Ethics: the big questions**, Blackwell Publishers, Oxford

Stokes, D. (2002), **Marketing**, (3rd Ed), Continuum, London

Sun, T., Horn, M. & Merritt, D. (2004), **Values and lifestyles of individualists and collectivists: a study on Chinese, Japanese, British and US consumers**, *Journal of Consumer Marketing*, Vol.21 No 5 pp.318-331

Taylor, S.A., Celuch, K. & Goodwin, S. (2004), **The importance of brand equity to customer loyalty**, *Journal of Product and Brand Management*, Vol.13 No 4 pp.217-227

Thomas, J.R. & Nelson, J.K. (1996), **Research Methods in Physical Activity**, (3rd Ed.), Human Kinetics, Leeds

Thomson, A. (2003), **Critical Reasoning**, (2nd Ed.), Routledge, London

Vernon, M.D. (1971), **Human Motivation**, (2nd Ed), Cambridge University Press, London

Whiteman, P. (1999), **Understanding Medicine; how it works for you**, (5th Ed), Hodder & Stoughton, UK

Yam-Tang, E.P.Y. & Chan, R.Y.K. (1998), **Purchasing behaviours and perceptions of environmentally harmful products**, *Marketing Intelligence & Planning*, Vol.16 No6 pp.356-362

Ethical Consumer (2003), **Why buy ethically? An Introduction to the Philosophy Behind Ethical Purchasing**, www.ethicalconsumer.org

CAFOD, ChristianAid & SCIAF (2004), Youth Topics, www.cafod.org.uk, www.christianaid.org.uk, www.sciaf.org.uk

- **The New Testament, Psalms and Proverbs**, The Gideons International, Tennessee

www.consultancymarketing.co.uk/marketing-definition.htm

www.bcentral.co.uk/marketing/marketingbasics/a-definition-of-marketing.mspx

www.newconsumer.org

www.fairtrade.org

www.tradecraftshop.co.uk

www.uri.org.uk

www.ingramcontent.com/pod-product-compliance
Lightning Source LLC
Chambersburg PA
CBHW050009230526
45465CB00003BB/1337